PRAISE FOR DIABETES SNACKS, TREATS, & EASY EATS FOR KIDS

What a wonderful introduction to diabetic cooking for children and adolescents! These healthy recipes offer lots of variety and are creative and easy to follow. Children and adolescents with or without diabetes can benefit from this fun exploration of eating better.

—*Alisa Levine, M.P.H., R.D., L.D.*

Diabetes Snacks, Treats, and Easy Eats For Kids

130 Recipes for the Foods Kids Really Like to Eat

BARBARA GRUNES

WITH Linda R. Yoakam, R.D., M.S.

SURREY
BOOKS

CHICAGO

Surrey Books is an imprint of Agate Publishing, Inc.

Printed in the United States of America.

Diabetes Snacks, Treats, and Easy Eats for Kids, 2nd Edition
ISBN: 978-1-57284-109-3

Nutritional analyses: Linda R. Yoakam, R.D., M.S.

The Library of Congress has cataloged the first edition of this book as follows:

Library of Congress Cataloging-in-Publication Data:
Grunes, Barbara.
 Diabetes snacks, treats & easy eats for kids : 130 recipes for the foods kids really like to eat / Barbara Grunes, with Linda R. Yoakam.—1st U.S. ed.
 p. cm. Includes index. ISBN 1-57284-085-4
1. Diabetes in children—Diet therapy—Recipes. 2. Diabetes in adolescence—Diet therapy—Recipes. I. Yoakam, Linda R. II. Title. III. Title: Diabetes snacks, treats and easy eats for kids.
 RJ420.D5G78 2006 641.5'6314—dc22

2006010141

10 9 8 7 6 5 4 3 2

Agate and Surrey books are available in bulk at discount prices. For more information, go to agatepublishing.com.

DEDICATION

I would like to dedicate this book to the diabetics in my life: Edith Maniff, my mother; Jerome Grunes, M.D., my husband; Gary Maniff, my brother; Virginia Van Vynckt, my friend and fellow food writer.

And most recently, Reba Georgiadis, my daughter.

And to my consultants, my grandchildren: Avi, Marissa, Big Natalie, Claire, Suzie, Big Noah, Ethan, Natalie, and Noah.

CONTENTS

Introduction   ix

CHAPTER ONE
Snacks   1
Pizza Puffs   2
Toasted Cheese Roll-Ups   3
Pumpkin-Face English Muffins   4
Pizza Dough Alphabet   5
Cinnamon Toast   6
Johnny Cakes   7
Peanut Butter and Jelly   8
Pretzel Nuggets
Stuffed Mini Pitas   9
Scrambled Egg Whites   10
Super Bowl Chicken "Wings"   11
Ranch Sauce   12
Chicken Nugget Strips   13
Trail Mix   14
Cereal Toss   15
Frozen Fudge Pops   16
Juicicles   17
Grilled Fruit   18
Sensationally Easy Warm   19
Pineapple Slices
Island Fruit Dip   20
Sweet Potato Chips with Fresh   21
Tomato Salsa
Fresh Tomato Salsa   22
Buttered Popcorn   23
Do-It-Yourself Munchies   24
After-School Snacking Cake   25
TV Snack Special: Nachos Grandes   26
Lunch Box Yellow Cake   27

CHAPTER TWO
Breakfast and Lunch   29
Vegetable Pancakes   30
Puffy German Pancake   31
Chinese Eggs   32
Eggs in a Hole   33
Banana-Stuffed French Toast   34
The Best French Toast with Very   35

Berry Sauce
Very Berry Sauce   36
Buttermilk Waffles   37
Nutty Waffles   38
Crepes   39
Breakfast A-Go Go   40
Peaches in Blankets   41
Spud Pancakes with Sour Cream   42
Crustless Carrot Quiche   43

CHAPTER THREE
Pizza, Pasta, and Grains   45
Whole-Wheat Pizza Cut-Outs   46
Whole-Wheat Pizza Crust   47
Pizza Christmas Trees   48
Mexican Pizza   49
Molded Angel Hair Pasta   50
True Grits   51
Orzo Salad   52
Ziti with Fresh Tomato Sauce   53
Elbow Macaroni Salad   54
Zingy Marinara Sauce on a Bed   55
of Noodles
Marinara Sauce   56
Pinenutty Thai Pasta   57

CHAPTER FOUR
Sandwiches and Salads   59
Grilled Cheese Sandwich   60
Southwest Scrambled Egg
Tortilla Wrap   61
Chicken Fajitas   62
Shrimp Quesadillas   63
Turkey Quesadillas   64
Gooey Sloppy Joes   65
Rocky Shore Tuna Roll   66
Egg Salad Stuffed in a Horn   67
Garbage Salad   68
Yogurt Herb Dressing   68
Taco Salad   69
Blueberry Salad   70
Green Dressing   71

Far East Salad in Radicchio Cups 72
Grilled Fruit Salad with Pineapple Chutney 73
Pineapple Chutney (For Teenagers) 74
White and Green Potato Salad 75
Thai Salad 76

CHAPTER FIVE
Sides and Soups 77
Nutty Cole Slaw 78
Stir-Fried Noodle Pudding 79
Tossed Corn off the Cob 80
Baked Sweet Potatoes 81
Shrimp on a Stick 82
Mushy Peas 83
Stir-Fried Vegetables 84
Tomato Popcorn Soup 85
10-Minute Popeye Soup 86
Summer Cantaloupe Soup in a Shell 87
Won Ton Soup 88
Chili Soup 89

CHAPTER SIX
Main Dishes 91
Fried Tortellini 92
Dinosaur Meatballs 93
Easy Arroz con Pollo (Chicken 94
with Rice)
Campfire Chicken and 95
Roasted Potatoes
Chili Spice 95
Roasted Potatoes 96
Veggie Frittata 97
Eggs with Lox and Onion 98
Greek Chicken 99
Grilled Burger with All 100
the Trimmings
Piled-High Baked Potatoes 101
Customized Rotisserie Chicken 102
Turkey Pick-up Sticks 103
Fish Strips 104
Cowboy Bill's Turkey Chili 105
Chicken Sausages with Apples 106
Homemade Turkey Sausages 107
Aloha Chicken 108
Home Fries 109
California Rolls with Turkey 110

CHAPTER SEVEN
Muffins and Cupcakes 111
Blueberry Muffins with Bunny Ears 112
Cocoa Muffins 113
Chocolate Chip Muffin Tops 114

Popovers 115
Angel Cupcakes 116
Cherry Cupcakes 117
Mini Chocolate Cupcakes 118
Ice Cream Cone Cupcakes 119

CHAPTER EIGHT
Sweet Treats and Desserts 121
Apple Betty Pie 122
Raspberry Applesauce 123
Graham Cracker Crust 124
Single Pie Crust 125
Gingersnap Crust 126
Fruit Turnovers 127
Pear Grunt 128
Country Apple Pie 129
Crustless Custard Fruit Pie 130
Star-Topped Fruit Salad 131
No-Bake Strawberry Cheesecakes 132
Ice Cream Sandwiches 133
The Quickest Rice Pudding 134
Individual Noodle Puddings 135
Banana Cream Pie 136
Chocolate Waffles 137
Vanilla Tapioca Pudding 138
"Wormy" Apples on a Stick 139
Apples on a Stick Drizzled 140
with Chocolate
Strawberry Sundaes 141
Individual Chocolate Cakes 142
Flourless Chocolate Cake 143
Frozen Lemon Yogurt 144
Jelly Bean Tarts 145
Toasted Angel Cake with Raspberries 146
Cream Soda Float 147
Tea Party Peach Melba Cakes 148
Raspberry Sauce 149
Wiggly, Slimy, Wormy Gelatin 150
Waffle Scoops and Plum Sauce 151
Washington's Birthday Cherry Treat 152
Dessert Pizza 153
Mint Meringue Shells for Christmas 154
Crunchy Vanilla Cookies for 155
After-School Snacking
Oatmeal Nuggets 156
Flan 157

Index 158

INTRODUCTION

DIABETES IS A DIFFICULT DISEASE for anyone to deal with. But it can be especially hard for children, and even more so for their parents, to live with diabetes in a culture that considers glorified cookies a breakfast food and where the typical restaurant children's meal is a hot dog and French fries. The child-friendly recipes you'll find here offer a positive—and tasty—alternative.

Like many American adults, too many children are overweight, sedentary, and diabetic. Today, children as young as 10 years old are being diagnosed with Type 2 diabetes, which used to be thought of as a disease of older adults. But with a poor diet and inactive lifestyle, children, too, are developing diabetes.

The good news is that life is easier for both adults and children with diabetes than it used to be. Improved medications, insulin delivery, and blood sugar monitoring technology make it easier to keep your child's blood sugar under control. A wealth of good-tasting, reduced-sugar, and no-sugar foods, plus tons of healthy convenience foods such as peeled baby carrots, bagged salads, and cut-up fruit, make it easy to plan healthful snacks and meals not only for your diabetic child but for your entire family. This recipe collection is designed to help you do just that.

Recommended diets for those with diabetes have loosened up a lot from the old days. For the most part, even sugary and rich foods are not forbidden. Children with diabetes can have sweets in moderate amounts as long as the sweet counts as part of their overall daily carbohydrate intake. Ten percent of one's total carbohydrates as sugary sweets is considered acceptable. These days, the child with diabetes can have her cake and eat it too, joining her non-diabetic friends at birthday parties and picnics.

Even though children with diabetes do not have to give up favorite dishes and snacks they like, you need to plan meals carefully, both for nutritional quality and quantity. Choose foods that are low in fat, low to moderate in carbohydrates, and higher in fiber. A healthy diet not only helps keep your child's blood sugar under better control now but helps him establish good eating habits that will serve him well as an adult.

It's very important that you consult frequently with your child's doctor and dietitian to make sure that his or her diet is meeting your youngster's needs. With their tendency to eat erratically and change food likes and dislikes often, kids even more than adults need a meal plan specially tailored to each individual as well as constant monitoring to make sure they follow it.

Balancing What They Eat

For people with diabetes, controlling carbohydrate intake can be of major importance since carbohydrates raise glucose levels faster and more dramatically than other foods. Carbohydrates are found in foods with natural or added sugar such as breads, pasta, rice, crackers, cereals, potatoes, fresh fruits and juices, milk, table sugar, jams, and jellies. Other foods contain carbohydrates in combination with proteins and fats; some examples are cakes, ice cream, doughnuts, pizza, potato chips, and soups.

Table sugar used to be a "forbidden" food. It is now allowed in small amounts when needed for taste or texture, as long as it is counted with the total carbohydrate intake. Many diabetic educators consider the total carbs more important than where they come from. Other researchers believe people with diabetes should eat less foods, such as potatoes and breads, that are high on the glycemic index, a scale used to rank the speed at which carbohydrates are converted to blood sugar.

At any rate, sugary foods often are also high in fat and lacking fiber. Fiber is important because it helps slow the rate at which your body digests and absorbs carbohydrates. Offer your child whole-wheat instead of white bread, corn or whole-wheat tortillas instead of regular flour tortillas, and fruit more often than fruit juice.

Portion control is crucial, especially if your child is overweight. Although it's outside the scope of this book, regular physical activity is also essential.

The Exchange System vs. Counting Carbs

A variety of meal-planning strategies can be used to control diabetes. Keep in mind that individualizing meal plans is the key to successful control of blood glucose levels. Even though meal planning for diabetes is really little more than establishing a healthy way of eating and people with diabetes today eat the same foods as people without diabetes, it is recommended that you see your registered dietitian for that all-important meal plan.

Two popular meal-planning strategies are in wide use among people with diabetes. One is the exchange system, in which foods are divided into six basic food groups according to the calories they contain and the sources of those calories. Foods in the same group with similar calorie sources can be exchanged, or substituted, for one another to meet the daily allowed quantity of that particular food group. A registered dietitian or certified diabetes educator can best help you decide how many exchanges, or servings, of which foods should be allowed at each meal.

Another method of meal planning for people with diabetes is to count the number of carbohydrate grams eaten. Units of insulin are then prescribed based on the number of carbohydrates consumed. The amount of carbohydrates per unit of insulin is tailored to the individual with the help of a registered dietitian or certified diabetes educator.

Because of the growing popularity of carb counting, the grams of carbohydrates, as well as other nutritional values, are listed right along with each recipe in the book to help you stay within daily prescribed limits and yet allow your child to enjoy a wide variety of the snacks and foods kids love.

Note, too, that consistency, or routine intake, is very important. To keep blood sugar at optimum levels, try to make sure your child eats about the same quantity of food and in the same proportions of carbohydrate, protein, and fat at about the same time each day. You may need to make adjustments in the eating plan to allow for sick days or for increased or reduced activity.

Nutritional Information

Diabetes Snacks, Treats & Easy Eats for Kids offers a wide range of recipes from snacks, sandwiches, salads, soups, and main dishes to desserts. Each recipe is accompanied by nutritional information.

Today, preparing healthy meals is a snap thanks to a variety of new food products made with less fat, sodium, and sugar. Reduced-fat cheeses, low-sodium broth and canned goods, and sugar-free ice cream and instant pudding mixes are readily available. Lettuces and spinach are pre-washed and packaged for convenience; carrots and cabbage are shredded and packaged. In addition, flavorful low-sodium spice mixes abound, and there are a variety of sugar substitutes, from spoonable forms for baking to convenient single-serve packets, to help reduce total calorie and carbohydrate intake.

We use the sugar substitute sucralose, sold under the brand name Splenda No Calorie Sweetener, in many recipes in this book because it can be used in both cold and cooked foods, and children generally don't object to its taste. Egg substitute, nonfat whipped topping, and nonfat cooking spray are routinely called for to control dietary fat and cholesterol. Low-fat meats such as skinless chicken breasts, 90% lean ground beef, and pork tenderloin were selected instead of higher-fat cuts.

The recipes in *Diabetes Snacks, Treats & Easy Eats for Kids* were created using the highest quality ingredients available, and they often call for convenience products to save time. Eating sensibly should not have to mean extra time in the kitchen. Recipes also have been kept simple and easy. Where appropriate, let children enjoy the fun of helping in recipe preparation; it will give them more zest for the food they eat, not to mention fundamental cooking skills.

Recipes throughout the book reflect the nutritional standards and follow the guidelines recommended by the United States Department of Agriculture for the general population as well as for people with diabetes.

Nutritional analyses and exchanges provided for the recipes were calculated using an industry-standard nutritional software program. Nutritional information is meant to be used as a guideline only. Figures are based on laboratory values of ingredients, so results may vary slightly depending on the brand of ingredient used and the method of preparation. Other factors that can affect the accuracy of nutritional data include variability in sizes, weights, and measures of fruits, vegetables, and other foods.

Exchange values are based on averages of the foods within the group. If the carbohydrate content of a day's intake is estimated using the exchanges shown, there may be a difference between such estimates and the actual values consumed.

Ingredients noted as "optional," "to taste," or "as garnish" are not included in the nutritional information. When alternate choices or amounts of ingredients are given, or a range in the number of servings is shown, the ingredient, amount, or number of servings listed first has been used for analysis.

By following a healthy eating plan and increasing physical activity, most children can control their weight and the progress of diabetes. At the same time, they need not feel that they are different from other kids or have to eat different foods. As the recipes in this collection prove, the same healthy foods can be eaten—and enjoyed—by their family and friends.

Be sure to check with your child's doctor, registered dietitian, or certified diabetes educator to see how these recipes can fit into your child's individualized meal plan. Then serve the recipes with confidence to your entire family, knowing that everyone can enjoy familiar and delicious food together. After all, it's not about "good," "bad," or "forbidden" foods. It's about feeding your child and family sensibly, making sure everyone exercises regularly, and having fun.

Chapter One

Snacks

Serving pizza as small turnovers rather than slicing the whole pie makes it easy to control portions.

Pizza Puffs

MAKES 8 SERVINGS (2 PUFFS PER SERVING)

> 1 package whole-wheat pizza dough, or homemade crust (see recipe on page 47)
> Butter-flavored cooking spray
> 1 cup grated reduced-fat mozzarella
> ⅓ cup pizza sauce, or spaghetti sauce
> Italian seasoning herbs

Preheat oven to 425°F. Spray a cookie sheet.

Roll out dough thinly on lightly floured surface. Using a 2½-inch biscuit or cookie cutter, cut out 16 circles.

In a small bowl, mix together mozzarella and pizza sauce.

To fill pizza puffs, place a round of dough on a plate and spoon 1½ teaspoons of filling on bottom half. Fold top half over and seal edges tightly. Set on the cookie sheet. Continue until all puffs are completed. Spray puffs with cooking spray and sprinkle with Italian seasoning.

Bake in center of oven for 15 minutes or until dough is cooked through and filling is hot. Serve warm.

....

Per Serving: Calories: 87; % of calories from fat: 20; Fat (gm): 1.9; Saturated Fat (gm): 0.7; Cholesterol (mg): 3.8; Sodium (mg): 274; Protein (gm): 3.7; Carbohydrate (gm): 14 Exchanges: Milk: 0.0; Vegetable: 0.0; Fruit: 0.0; Bread: 1.0; Meat: 0.0; Fat: 0.5

Kids like foods in new fun forms—like a sandwich that's rolled instead of stacked. The cheese should be at room temperature. If it is too cold, it will crack when you roll it.

TOASTED CHEESE ROLL-UPS

MAKES 2 SERVINGS

 2 slices whole-wheat bread, crusts removed
 2 slices reduced-fat Swiss cheese
 Butter-flavored cooking spray

Place one bread slice on a plate. Trim one cheese slice to fit bread if necessary. Center cheese on bread. Roll up bread and cheese, jelly-roll style. Repeat for second slice of bread and cheese.

Heat a sprayed nonstick frying pan. Place cheese rolls seam side down in the pan. Heat and turn as they brown, about 1 minute in all.

Remove roll-ups to plates and serve.

....

Per Serving: Calories: 132; % of calories from fat: 31; Fat (gm): 4.6; Saturated Fat (gm): 2.2; Cholesterol (mg): 15; Sodium (mg): 173; Protein (gm): 10.5; Carbohydrate (gm): 12 Exchanges: Milk: 0.0; Vegetable: 0.0; Fruit: 0.0; Bread: 1.0; Meat: 1.0; Fat: 0.0

Halloween can be a tough holiday for kids with diabetes, but these cheery pumpkin faces give them something besides candy to focus on.

PUMPKIN-FACE ENGLISH MUFFINS

MAKES 2 SERVINGS

> 1 whole-wheat English muffin, split in half
> ¼ cup prepared pizza sauce, or to taste
> ⅓ cup grated reduced-fat mozzarella cheese
> 1 slice fat-free American cheese product

Preheat oven to 350°F. Use a nonstick cookie sheet.

Using a spoon, spread sauce evenly over the 2 muffin halves. Sprinkle muffin halves with mozzarella cheese.

Using a small paring knife, cut 4 pumpkin-like triangle eyes and 2 smiling mouths out of the American cheese. Arrange eyes and mouths over the mozzarella cheese on each muffin half.

Place muffin halves on the cookie sheet. Bake in center of oven for 5 minutes or until mozzarella cheese melts. You can easily double this recipe.

....

Per Serving: Calories: 137; % of calories from fat: 21; Fat (gm): 3.2; Saturated Fat (gm): 2; Cholesterol (mg): 10; Sodium (mg): 650; Protein (gm): 8.9; Carbohydrate (gm): 18 Exchanges: Milk: 0.0; Vegetable: 0.0; Fruit: 0.0; Bread: 1.0; Meat: 1.0; Fat: 0.0

For the best flavor, sprinkle these with a combination of poppy seeds, sesame seeds, and onion flakes—but only if the kids like "seedy" bread. It's fun to spell out the child's name with dough letters.

PIZZA DOUGH ALPHABET

MAKES 12 SERVINGS (1 LETTER PER SERVING)

Butter-flavored spray

Defrosted bread dough (preferably whole-wheat), or homemade
whole-wheat pizza dough (see recipe on page 47)

2 egg whites, lightly beaten

⅓ cup poppy seeds, sesame seeds, or dried onion flakes

Preheat oven to 350°F. Spray a cookie sheet.

Have children wash their hands. Divide dough into 12 pieces. Roll out dough into pencil-thick ropes. Shape each piece into a letter of the alphabet. Place letters on the cookie sheet.

Brush alphabet shapes with egg white and sprinkle with poppy seeds, sesame seeds, or dried onion flakes.

Bake in center of oven for 12 to 15 minutes or until just firm. Let cool.

....

Per Serving: Calories: 129; % of calories from fat: 23; Fat (gm): 3.2; Saturated Fat (gm): 0.2; Cholesterol (mg): 0; Sodium (mg): 222; Protein (gm): 5; Carbohydrate (gm): 19 Exchanges: Milk: 0.0; Vegetable: 0.0; Fruit: 0.0; Bread: 1.0; Meat: 0.0; Fat: 1.0

Cinnamon Toast can double for a breakfast dish or an after-school treat. Add a few raisins if you wish to make it more special.

CINNAMON TOAST

MAKES 2 SERVINGS

1 whole-wheat English muffin, split in half
½ cup reduced-fat cottage cheese
1 teaspoon Splenda No Calorie Sweetener, or sugar
½ teaspoon ground cinnamon

Preheat oven to 350°F. Use a nonstick cookie sheet.

Split muffin in half. Set aside.

In a small bowl, whisk together cottage cheese, Splenda No Calorie Sweetener, and cinnamon. Spread cottage cheese mixture over each muffin half.

Arrange muffins on cookie sheet and bake in center of oven for 5 minutes or until warmed through.

....

Per Serving: Calories: 109; % of calories from fat: 10; Fat (gm): 1.3; Saturated Fat (gm): 0.5; Cholesterol (mg): 2.3; Sodium (mg): 440; Protein (gm): 10; Carbohydrate (gm): 15.6 Exchanges: Milk: 0.0; Vegetable: 0.0; Fruit: 0.0; Bread: 1.0; Meat: 1.0; Fat: 0.0

The portable snack is nothing new. The early American colonists had the same idea. They would bake a pancake called a "Journey Cake" to take along on a trip. Somewhere along the line, a Journey Cake became a Johnny Cake. It still makes a good "take-along" snack. Our version is cut into squares for easier preparation.

JOHNNY CAKES

MAKES 16 SERVINGS

Butter-flavored cooking spray

1 cup all-purpose flour

1 cup white, or yellow, cornmeal

1¼ teaspoons baking soda

2 tablespoons Splenda No Calorie Sweetener, or sugar

¼ cup egg substitute, or 1 egg

1 cup reduced-fat buttermilk

3 tablespoons reduced-fat margarine, or butter, melted

Preheat oven to 400°F. Spray an 8 x 8-inch baking pan.

In a mixing bowl, whisk together the flour, cornmeal, baking soda, and sweetener. Stir in egg substitute, buttermilk, and melted margarine.

Pour batter into prepared pan, and bake in center of oven for 20 to 25 minutes or until a knife inserted into the center comes out clean. Cool cake and cut it into 16 squares. This is best served warm and spread with no-sugar-added fruit preserves, reduced-fat margarine, or butter.

Per Serving: Calories: 77; % of calories from fat: 16; Fat (gm): 1.4; Saturated Fat (gm): 0.3; Cholesterol (mg): 0.6; Sodium (mg): 148; Protein (gm): 2.4; Carbohydrate (gm): 13.7 Exchanges: Milk: 0.0; Vegetable: 0.0; Fruit: 0.0; Bread: 1.0; Meat: 0.0; Fat: 0.0

Add some entertainment value to plain old peanut butter and jelly by putting the spreads on pretzels instead of bread.

PEANUT BUTTER AND JELLY PRETZEL NUGGETS

MAKES 6 SERVINGS

6 pretzel nuggets, split in half
2 tablespoons smooth reduced-fat peanut butter
1 tablespoon no-sugar-added grape, or raspberry, jelly

Spread each pretzel nugget half with 1 teaspoon peanut butter and top with ½ teaspoon jelly.

....

Per Serving: Calories: 71; % of calories from fat: 26; Fat (gm): 2; Saturated Fat (gm): 0.4; Cholesterol (mg): 0; Sodium (mg): 57; Protein (gm): 2.3; Carbohydrate (gm): 10.6 Exchanges: Milk: 0.0; Vegetable: 0.0; Fruit: 0.0; Bread: 1.0; Meat: 0.0; Fat: 0.0

Mini pitas are a great size for an after-school snack. If your child does not like strong flavors, you can substitute low-fat mozzarella for the feta cheese and chopped almonds for the olives.

STUFFED MINI PITAS

MAKES 6 SERVINGS (1 PITA PER SERVING)

½ cup chopped tomato
¼ cup crumbled feta cheese
2 tablespoons chopped, pitted black olives*
½ cup chopped lettuce
6 whole-wheat mini pita pockets

In a bowl, combine tomato, feta, black olives, and lettuce. Warm and open each pita. Divide filling and stuff each pocket.

*Omit olives if serving young children.

Per Serving: Calories: 88; % of calories from fat: 20; Fat (gm): 2.2; Saturated Fat (gm): 1; Cholesterol (mg): 5.6; Sodium (mg): 250; Protein (gm): 4.6; Carbohydrate (gm): 15 Exchanges: Milk: 0.0; Vegetable: 0.0; Fruit: 0.0; Bread: 1.0; Meat: 0.0; Fat: 0.5

I dropped in to visit my grandchildren one day and saw that Avi (a junior in high school) was busy making himself scrambled egg whites. What a good idea, I thought.

SCRAMBLED EGG WHITES

MAKES 2 SERVINGS

> 1 tablespoon reduced-fat margarine, or butter
> Butter-flavored cooking spray
> ½ cup chopped onion
> 4 egg whites, lightly beaten
> Salt and white pepper, to taste

Melt margarine in a sprayed nonstick frying pan over medium heat.

Add the onions and cook until soft, about 3 minutes, stirring occasionally. If pan seems dry, spray again.

Stir in egg whites. Reduce heat to low, and scramble eggs until cooked through but not dry. Season with salt and white pepper.

Per Serving: Calories: 76; % of calories from fat: 35; Fat (gm): 2.9; Saturated Fat (gm): 0.4; Cholesterol (mg): 0; Sodium (mg): 181; Protein (gm): 7.7; Carbohydrate (gm): 4.6 Exchanges: Milk: 0.0; Vegetable: 0.0; Fruit: 0.0; Bread: 0.0; Meat: 1.0; Fat: 2.0

Thanks to the skin and blue cheese dressing, traditional chicken wings are high in fat. This slimmed-down alternative tastes great and is much better for kids and adults alike.

SUPER BOWL CHICKEN "WINGS"

MAKES 24 "WINGS" (8 SERVINGS)

½ cup lemon juice

2 tablespoons grated fresh ginger

2 cloves garlic, minced

¼ cup canola oil

4 skinless, boneless chicken thighs

6 stalks celery

Ranch Sauce (recipe follows)

Cooking spray

1 tablespoon barbecue sauce

Make marinade in a glass bowl or self-sealing plastic bag by combining lemon juice, ginger, and garlic. Add canola oil and whisk or shake to incorporate.

Cut each chicken thigh into 6 strips.

Add chicken strips to marinade and turn so that they are all touched by the marinade. Cover or seal and marinate for 2 to 4 hours. Drain, discarding marinade.

While chicken is marinating, prepare celery sticks and Ranch Sauce, and refrigerate until needed.

....

COMPLETE RECIPE Per Serving: Calories: 177; % of calories from fat: 52; Fat (gm): 9; Saturated Fat (gm): 1; Cholesterol (mg): 47.6; Sodium (mg): 197; Protein (gm): 13; Carbohydrate (gm): 5.7 Exchanges: Milk: 0.0; Vegetable: 0.0; Fruit: 0.0; Bread: 0.6; Meat: 2.0; Fat: 0.5

To prepare celery, cut each stalk in half, then cut halves vertically into thirds, to make 36 pieces of celery in all.

Heat a sprayed nonstick frying pan over medium heat. Cook chicken strips a few minutes, turning as they cook so they are crisp on all sides. As chicken strips are cooking, brush lightly with barbecue sauce. Make sure chicken is cooked through.

Arrange chicken strip "wings" on a serving dish with celery sticks and Ranch Sauce for dipping.

RANCH SAUCE

MAKES 8 SERVINGS

> 1 cup plain fat-free yogurt
>
> 1 tablespoon dried ranch seasoning, or sugar-free ranch salad dressing
>
> 1 tablespoon grated lemon peel, optional

In a small bowl, combine yogurt, ranch seasoning or dressing, and lemon peel. Cover and refrigerate until ready to serve. Stir again before serving.

....

RANCH SAUCE ONLY Per Serving: Calories: 40; % of calories from fat: 3; Fat (gm): 0.1; Saturated Fat (gm): 0.1; Cholesterol (mg): 0.6; Sodium (mg): 134; Protein (gm): 1.8; Carbohydrate (gm): 3 Exchanges: Milk: 0.0; Vegetable: 0.0; Fruit: 0.0; Bread: 0.5; Meat: 0.0; Fat: 0.0

Banish those greasy fast-food chicken nuggets and say hello to their tasty, healthier cousins.

Chicken Nugget Strips

MAKES 8 SERVINGS

1 whole skinless, boneless chicken breast
½ cup whole-wheat flour
½ cup egg substitute
½ cup reduced-fat buttermilk
¾ cup dry bread crumbs, or crushed corn flakes
Salt, pepper, and garlic powder, to taste
Butter-flavored cooking spray

Preheat oven to 450°F. Use a nonstick cookie sheet.

Slice chicken into ½-inch-wide strips and set aside.

Put flour in a small bowl. In another small bowl, mix egg substitute and buttermilk together. In a third bowl, combine the crumbs with salt, pepper, and garlic powder.

Roll each chicken strip lightly in flour, then dip into egg-buttermilk mixture, and finally roll in seasoned crumbs. Arrange strips on sprayed cookie sheet. Bake for 20 minutes, turning once, or until chicken is cooked through. Remove one strip and cut to check for doneness. Serve immediately.

Per Serving: Calories: 154; % of calories from fat: 10; Fat (gm): 1.7; Saturated Fat (gm): 0.4; Cholesterol (mg): 33.5; Sodium (mg): 174; Protein (gm): 17.9; Carbohydrate (gm): 16.1
Exchanges: Milk: 0.0; Vegetable: 0.0; Fruit: 0.0; Bread: 1.0; Meat: 2.0; Fat: 0.0

A small bag of trail mix makes a great lunch box treat or after-school snack. Customize it by using your family's favorite fruits and nuts. Even young children can toss together the ingredients.

TRAIL MIX

MAKES 2 CUPS (8 SERVINGS)

½ cup raisins

½ cup banana chips

½ cup crumbled sugar-free oatmeal, or coconut, cookies

½ cup sliced almonds, or pine nuts

Toss raisins, banana chips, crumbled cookies, and pine nuts in a bowl.

Store Trail Mix in a covered jar or in self-sealing plastic bags.

....

Per Serving: Calories: 137; % of calories from fat: 44; Fat (gm): 7.3; Saturated Fat (gm): 2.2; Cholesterol (mg): 0; Sodium (mg): 36; Protein (gm): 2.7; Carbohydrate (gm): 17.8 Exchanges: Milk: 0.0; Vegetable: 0.0; Fruit: 0.0; Bread: 1.0; Meat: 0.0; Fat: 1.5

Vary the cereal and nuts in this recipe to create the flavors and textures your family prefers. If you're serving this—or any other dish with peanuts—to guests, make sure no one has peanut allergies.

CEREAL TOSS

MAKES 20 SERVINGS (½ CUP PER SERVING)

Butter-flavored cooking spray
4 cups Chex cereal (or any cold cereal combination)
2 cups Goldfish crackers
1 cup peanuts
3 cups thin pretzels
3 tablespoons reduced-calorie margarine, melted
1 tablespoon Worcestershire sauce
½ teaspoon seasoned salt
½ teaspoon garlic powder

Preheat oven to 375°F. Spray a cookie sheet.

In a large bowl, mix together cereal, Goldfish, peanuts, and pretzels. Mix margarine, Worcestershire, seasoned salt, and garlic powder, then toss with cereal mixture until evenly coated. Spread mixture on sprayed cookie sheet. Bake in center of oven for 20 minutes or until toasted and crisp.

Spoon mixture into a large bowl. Serve Cereal Toss in individual paper cups.

Per Serving: Calories: 133; % of calories from fat: 38; Fat (gm): 5.7; Saturated Fat (gm): 0.9; Cholesterol (mg): 1.7; Sodium (mg): 287; Protein (gm): 3.4; Carbohydrate (gm): 17.4 Exchanges: Milk: 0.0; Vegetable: 0.0; Fruit: 0.0; Bread: 1.0; Meat: 0.0; Fat: 1.0

Besides cocoa, you can freeze sugar-free yogurt, juice, or diet soda to make pops. You can easily double this recipe. To make an Italian ice, remove the frozen cocoa and allow it to soften slightly. Spoon chunks of cocoa into a food processor and process a few seconds to make slush. Spoon into pointed cups and serve immediately.

FROZEN FUDGE POPS

MAKES 8 SERVINGS

> 2 packages (.29 ounce each) diet, or sugar-free, hot cocoa mix
> 2 cups hot, not boiling, water
> 1 ice cube tray
> Wooden craft sticks (available at craft stores)

Empty packets of cocoa mix into a bowl. Add hot water. Whisk the mix and water until smooth. Cool.

Pour cooled cocoa into an ice cube tray to make 8 cubes. Place tray in freezer for 1 hour or until cocoa is almost firm. Insert wooden stick in each pop. Continue freezing until firm, about 3 hours.

You can also remove the pops from the ice cube tray, place them in a self-sealing plastic bag, and freeze. Remove one or two pops at a time as needed.

Per Serving: Calories: 14; % of calories from fat: 7; Fat (gm): 0.1; Saturated Fat (gm): 0.1; Cholesterol (mg): 0.7; Sodium (mg): 36; Protein (gm): 1.1; Carbohydrate (gm): 2.1 Exchanges: Milk: 0.0; Vegetable: 0.0; Fruit: 0.0; Bread: 0.0; Meat: 0.0; Fat: 0.0

Surprise the family with different choices of juice. Use funny straws decorated with cartoon characters for more fun. The Juicicles can also be served in an ice cream cup.

JUICICLES

MAKES 6 SERVINGS

3 cups orange juice

3 slushy cups, or paper cups

6 straws

Pour orange juice into a shallow bowl and freeze, about 2 hours. Let stand at room temperature for 10 minutes or until it is beginning to soften. Break juice mixture into chunks and place in a food processor. Puree. Return juice mixture to bowl and refreeze.

When ready to serve, again let juice begin to soften, about 10 minutes. Again puree frozen juice in food processor for a few seconds. Spoon immediately into slushy cups or paper cups. Serve immediately with a colorful straw or spoon.

....

Per Serving: Calories: 56; % of calories from fat: 4; Fat (gm): 0.2; Saturated Fat (gm): 0.03; Cholesterol (mg): 0; Sodium (mg): 1; Protein (gm): .9; Carbohydrate (gm): 12.9 Exchanges: Milk: 0.0; Vegetable: 0.0; Fruit: 1.0; Bread: 0.0; Meat: 0.0; Fat: 0.0

GRILLED FRUIT

MAKES 6 SERVINGS

Butter-flavored cooking spray
1 banana, peeled
6 1-inch-wide wedges of peeled cantaloupe
1 firm ripe pear, cored and halved

Spray fruit with cooking spray. Grill in a stovetop grill according to manufacturer's directions or cook, cut side down, on an outdoor grill using a grill screen.

Grill fruit only 1 to 2 minutes, until warm and softened.

Remove fruit from grill. Slice banana and pear. Arrange on individual plates with cantaloupe wedges and serve warm.

You can dress up this treat for special occasions with a small scoop of sugar-free vanilla ice cream.

....

Per Serving: Calories: 54; % of calories from fat: 3; Fat (gm): 0.2; Saturated Fat (gm): 0.1; Cholesterol (mg): 0; Sodium (mg): 10; Protein (gm): 0.8; Carbohydrate (gm): 13.6 Exchanges: Milk: 0.0; Vegetable: 0.0; Fruit: 1.0; Bread: 0.0; Meat: 0.0; Fat: 0.0

You'll love pineapple on the grill! Spray with butter-flavored cooking spray, and grill for 1 minute on each side.

SENSATIONALLY EASY WARM PINEAPPLE SLICES

MAKES 4 SERVINGS

2 tablespoons reduced-fat margarine, or butter
4 slices peeled fresh pineapple
1 tablespoon Splenda brown sugar blend

Melt margarine in a frying pan over medium heat. Add the pineapple slices, and fry them about 1 minute or just until they begin to turn golden. Using a spatula, turn pineapple over and continue cooking for another 1 to 2 minutes until golden on both sides.

Remove to individual serving dishes, sprinkle with brown sugar blend, and serve immediately.

Per Serving: Calories: 65; % of calories from fat: 36; Fat (gm): 3; Saturated Fat (gm): 0.4; Cholesterol (mg): 0; Sodium (mg): 70; Protein (gm): 0.5; Carbohydrate (gm): 11 Exchanges: Milk: 0.0; Vegetable: 0.0; Fruit:1.0; Bread: 0.0; Meat: 0.0; Fat: 0.5

For a new twist, serve fruits instead of vegetables with dip. Vary the fruit according to the season: tangerine segments in the winter, sliced apples or pears in the fall, sliced melon in the summer, and sliced pineapple in the spring.

Island Fruit Dip

MAKES 3 CUPS (6 SERVINGS)

3 cups plain fat-free yogurt
¼ cup mango chutney (or another flavor of your choice)
1 tablespoon finely chopped green onion
1¼ teaspoons mild curry powder

In a bowl, blend together yogurt, chutney, onion, and curry powder.

Spoon into a dipping bowl and surround with fruit slices. This is best served chilled.

....

Per Serving: Calories: 87; % of calories from fat: 3; Fat (gm): 0.3; Saturated Fat (gm): 0.2; Cholesterol (mg): 2.5; Sodium (mg): 122; Protein (gm): 7.2; Carbohydrate (gm): 14 Exchanges: Milk: 0.5; Vegetable: 0.0; Fruit: 0.5; Bread: 0.0; Meat: 0.0; Fat: 0.0

Use an indoor stove-top grill for this recipe or pan fry the potatoes in a sprayed nonstick frying pan. If potatoes stick to pan, add 1 to 2 tablespoons of reduced-fat margarine.

SWEET POTATO CHIPS WITH FRESH TOMATO SALSA

MAKES 6 SERVINGS

> 3 medium-large sweet potatoes, peeled
> Butter-flavored cooking spray
> ½ teaspoon garlic powder
> ½ teaspoon ground cinnamon
> Salt to taste
> 1½ cups Fresh Tomato Salsa (recipe follows)

Cut sweet potatoes in half and place them in a large saucepan filled with salted water. Bring to a boil, reduce heat, and cook over medium heat for 15 to 20 minutes or until potatoes are fork tender but still firm. Drain and cool.

Slice sweet potatoes ½ inch thick and transfer to a plate. Spray potatoes and sprinkle with garlic powder, cinnamon, and salt.

Spray a frying pan or stove-top grill. Cook sweet potatoes for 3 minutes, turning as needed, until potatoes are warm on the inside and crisp on the outside.

Remove potatoes to a serving dish. Pass Salsa in separate bowl.

··

COMPLETE RECIPE Per Serving: Calories: 87; % of calories from fat: 2; Fat (gm): 0.2; Saturated Fat (gm): 0; Cholesterol (mg): 0; Sodium (mg): 48.4; Protein (gm): 2; Carbohydrate (gm): 20 Exchanges: Milk: 0.0; Vegetable: 1.0; Fruit: 0.0; Bread: 1.0; Meat: 0.0; Fat: 0.0

If you are serving teenagers, you may want to add 1 jalapeño pepper, seeded and minced.

FRESH TOMATO SALSA

MAKES ABOUT 1 ½ CUPS (6 SERVINGS)

3 large, ripe tomatoes, chopped
½ cup minced red onion
¼ cup minced fresh cilantro, or to taste
Salt to taste

In a large bowl, toss tomatoes, onions, and cilantro together. Season to taste with salt.

Cover bowl and refrigerate until serving time and stir just before serving.

....

FRESH TOMATO SALSA ONLY Per Serving: Calories: 15; % of calories from fat: 7; Fat (gm): 0.1; Saturated Fat (gm): 0; Cholesterol (mg): 0; Sodium (mg): 3; Protein (gm): 0.6; Carbohydrate (gm): 3.4 Exchanges: Milk: 0.0; Vegetable: 0.0; Fruit: 0.0; Bread: 0.0; Meat: 0.0; Fat: 0.0

Who among us can resist buttered popcorn? To pop corn, simply place ¼ cup unpopped corn in an unprinted brown bag. Seal and microwave on High for 3 to 4 minutes. Do not overpop.

BUTTERED POPCORN

MAKES 6 SERVINGS

6 cups of plain popped corn (see instructions above)
2 tablespoons reduced-fat margarine, or butter, melted
½ teaspoon salt

In a large bowl, toss the popcorn with the margarine and salt until combined.

Serve immediately.

Per Serving: Calories: 47; % of calories from fat: 41; Fat (gm): 2.2; Saturated Fat (gm): 0.4; Cholesterol (mg): 0; Sodium (mg): 240; Protein (gm): 1; Carbohydrate (gm): 6.2 Exchanges: Milk: 0.0; Vegetable: 0.0; Fruit: 0.0; Bread: 0.5; Meat: 0.0; Fat: 0.0

Do-It-Yourself Munchies

MAKES 6 SERVINGS (3 CRACKERS PLUS TOPPINGS PER
SERVING)

    18 crackers

    9 cherry tomatoes, cut into halves

    1 cucumber, thinly sliced into 18 pieces

    2 hard-boiled eggs, each sliced into 9 pieces

    1 zucchini, thinly sliced into 18 pieces

Use other assorted raw cut vegetables, such as pepper strips and cooked asparagus tips, if desired.

Serve three crackers on each plate. Place sliced eggs and vegetables on individual plates, and let children decorate their own crackers.

....

Per Serving: Calories: 88; % of calories from fat: 42; Fat (gm): 4; Saturated Fat (gm): 0.9; Cholesterol (mg): 70.7; Sodium (mg): 102; Protein (gm): 4; Carbohydrate (gm): 9.6 Exchanges: Milk: 0.0; Vegetable: 0.0; Fruit: 0.0; Bread: 0.5; Meat: 0.0; Fat: 1.0

After-School Snacking Cake

MAKES 8 SERVINGS

Butter-flavored cooking spray

¼ cup egg substitute

¾ cup nonfat milk

1½ cups all-purpose flour

¾ cup Splenda No Calorie Sweetener

2 teaspoons baking powder

3 tablespoons currants

¾ teaspoon ground cinnamon

¼ teaspoon nutmeg

Preheat oven to 350°F. Spray an 8 x 8-inch nonstick cake pan.

In bowl of electric mixer, combine egg substitute and milk. Mix in flour, Splenda, and baking powder. Stir in currants, cinnamon, and nutmeg.

Pour batter into prepared pan. Bake in center of oven for 35 minutes or until a cake tester or toothpick inserted in center of cake comes out clean. Cool 5 minutes. Remove cake in slices; cool completely.

Per Serving: Calories: 100; % of calories from fat: 2; Fat (gm): 0.3; Saturated Fat (gm): 0.1; Cholesterol (mg): 0.5; Sodium (mg): 146; Protein (gm): 4; Carbohydrate (gm): 22.3 Exchanges: Milk: 0.0; Vegetable: 0.0; Fruit: 0.0; Bread: 1.5; Meat: 0.0; Fat: 0.0

TV Snack Special: Nachos Grandes

MAKES 12 SERVINGS

1 bag (16 ounces) baked tortilla chips
1 cup reduced-fat shredded mozzarella cheese
1 cup plain fat-free yogurt, or sour cream
1 cup Fresh Tomato Salsa (see recipe page 22)

Preheat oven to 375°F.

Place chips in a pie plate. Sprinkle with shredded cheese. Bake in center of oven for 5 minutes or until cheese has melted.

Using pot holders, remove pie plate from oven and allow to cool. Serve in pie plate with bowls of yogurt and salsa for dipping.

....

Per Serving: Calories: 183; % of calories from fat: 19; Fat (gm): 4; Saturated Fat (gm): 1; Cholesterol (mg): 5.4; Sodium (mg): 285; Protein (gm): 6.9; Carbohydrate (gm): 32 Exchanges: Milk: 0.0; Vegetable: 0.0; Fruit: 0.0; Bread: 2.0; Meat: 0.0; Fat: 1.0

LUNCH BOX YELLOW CAKE

MAKES 16 PIECES (1 PC. PER SERVING)

    Butter-flavored spray
    1 package (18.25 ounces) yellow cake mix
    1⅓ cups water
    ⅓ cup plain fat-free yogurt
    ¾ cup egg substitute
    2 cups frozen blueberries, defrosted, including juice

Preheat oven to 350°F. Spray a 7½ x 11-inch baking pan.

In large bowl of electric mixer, beat together cake mix, 1⅓ cups water, yogurt, and egg substitute. Mix for only 1 to 2 minutes or until combined; do not overmix. Batter should be smooth.

Pour batter into prepared pan. Smooth with a spatula.

Bake cake in center of oven for 30 to 35 minutes or until a tester or toothpick inserted in center of cake comes out dry.

Cool cake on rack. Cut into 16 even pieces and remove to serving plate, using a small spatula. Top with blueberries.

Other options are to sprinkle very lightly with confectioner's sugar or serve with 2 teaspoons of fat-free whipped topping and/or a few berries. Another possibility is to spread 1 teaspoon of apricot filling over the top of each cake piece before serving. Or serve plain in the lunch box.

Per Serving: Calories: 158; % of calories from fat: 22; Fat (gm): 3.9; Saturated Fat (gm): 0.6; Cholesterol (mg): 0.7; Sodium (mg): 238; Protein (gm): 3; Carbohydrate (gm): 28 Exchanges: Milk: 0.0; Vegetable: 0.0; Fruit: 0.0; Bread: 2.0; Meat: 0.0; Fat: 0.5

CHAPTER TWO

BREAKFAST AND LUNCH

For a crunchy texture and nutty flavor, sprinkle the pancakes lightly with sesame seeds or finely chopped almonds before turning.

VEGETABLE PANCAKES

MAKES 6 SERVINGS

¼ cup egg substitute, or 1 egg

½ cup all-purpose flour

½ cup whole-wheat flour

1 tablespoon baking powder

¾ cup reduced-fat milk

1 cup grated zucchini

1 cup grated carrots

Butter-flavored cooking spray

In a mixing bowl, whisk together egg substitute, flours, and baking powder. Whisk in milk, then stir in vegetables. Let stand 20 minutes.

Coat a large nonstick frying pan with cooking spray, and heat it over medium heat. Pour batter from a measuring cup or small pitcher into the pan to make pancakes of desired size. When bubbles form on top, turn over with a spatula. Continue cooking just until golden on both sides.

Serve with sugar-free maple syrup if desired.

....

Per Serving: Calories: 105; % of calories from fat: 8; Fat (gm): 1; Saturated Fat (gm): 0.4; Cholesterol (mg): 2.4; Sodium (mg): 292; Protein (gm): 4.9; Carbohydrate (gm): 20 Exchanges: Milk: 0.0; Vegetable: 1.0; Fruit: 0.0; Bread: 1.0; Meat: 0.0; Fat: 0.0

Puffy pancakes, which are really giant popovers, are fun to make and eat. Plus, they're lower in carbohydrates than the standard pancake.

PUFFY GERMAN PANCAKE

MAKES 4 SERVINGS

¾ cup egg substitute

½ cup reduced-fat milk

½ cup all-purpose flour

1 tablespoon Splenda No Calorie Sweetener, or sugar

1 tablespoon reduced-fat margarine, or butter

Preheat oven to 425°F.

In a bowl, combine egg substitute, milk, flour, and sweetener just until smooth.

Place margarine in a 9-inch pie plate. Put in the oven for 3 to 4 minutes, until the margarine is melted and the pie plate is hot. Working quickly, pour the batter into the hot pie plate.

Bake on upper rack of oven for 15 minutes or until puffed and lightly browned.

You can very lightly sprinkle the pancake with confectioner's sugar, and/or serve with Very Berry Sauce (see recipe on page 36).

....

Per Serving: Calories: 107; % of calories from fat: 18; Fat (gm): 2; Saturated Fat (gm): 0.7; Cholesterol (mg): 2.4; Sodium (mg): 134; Protein (gm): 7.1; Carbohydrate (gm): 14.5 Exchanges: Milk: 0.0; Vegetable: 0.0; Fruit: 0.0; Bread: 1.0; Meat: 0.5; Fat: 0.0

When our daughter Dorothy was very young, she just would not eat eggs. One lunchtime, my husband made scrambled eggs in the wok. Maybe because her father made them, Dorothy just loved those eggs, which our family quickly dubbed "Chinese Eggs."

To add an Asian flavor, include a bit of soy sauce or add some chopped water chestnuts or bamboo shoots.

CHINESE EGGS

MAKES 4 SERVINGS

1½ cups egg substitute
¼ cup reduced-fat milk
1 tablespoon vegetable oil, or canola oil
Cooking spray
¼ teaspoon salt

In a bowl, lightly beat egg substitute with milk.

Heat oil in a wok or nonstick frying pan coated with cooking spray. Sprinkle pan with salt. Add eggs to the pan. Using a wooden spoon, stir eggs as they begin to set.

Continue cooking and stirring occasionally until eggs are just cooked through. Do not overcook. Spoon eggs onto individual plates and serve hot.

....

Per Serving: Calories: 83; % of calories from fat: 42; Fat (gm): 3.7; Saturated Fat (gm): 0.6; Cholesterol (mg): 1.2; Sodium (mg): 324; Protein (gm): 9.5; Carbohydrate (gm): 2.2 Exchanges: Milk: 0.0; Vegetable: 0.0; Fruit: 0.0; Bread: 0.0; Meat: 1.5; Fat: 0.0

One young teenage friend of ours saw Olympia Dukakis making this dish in the movie "Moonstruck" and immediately asked her mom to show her how to make it. Kids are intrigued by these self-contained egg "sandwiches."

EGGS IN A HOLE

MAKES 4 SERVINGS

4 slices whole-wheat bread, crusts removed
2 tablespoons reduced-fat margarine, or butter
Butter-flavored cooking spray
4 eggs

Using a cookie cutter, cut out a 2–inch hole from the center of each slice of bread. Discard the cut-out centers, or reserve for another use.

Melt margarine or butter in a sprayed, large nonstick frying pan over medium heat. Add bread and fry for 1 minute or until lightly toasted. Turn bread over, using a spatula.

Working quickly, crack open each egg and pour it into the open center of each slice of bread. Fry until eggs are cooked through, 3 to 4 minutes. Serve on individual plates.

Per Serving: Calories: 160; % of calories from fat: 49; Fat (gm): 8.8; Saturated Fat (gm): 2.3; Cholesterol (mg): 211.5; Sodium (mg): 271; Protein (gm): 8.8; Carbohydrate (gm): 11.9 Exchanges: Milk: 0.0; Vegetable: 0.0; Fruit: 0.0; Bread: 1.0; Meat: 1.0; Fat: 1.0

Any child with a sweet tooth will love this breakfast treat.

BANANA-STUFFED FRENCH TOAST

MAKES 8 SERVINGS

4 slices, about 1-inch thick, day-old French bread, or whole-wheat bread

1 medium-large banana, sliced

¾ cup egg substitute, or 3 eggs

2 cups nonfat milk

1 teaspoon vanilla extract

2 tablespoons reduced-fat margarine, or butter

Butter-flavored cooking spray

Cut each bread slice in half. Slice a pocket in center of each piece of bread. Stuff banana slices in pocket. Set aside.

Whisk together egg substitute, milk, and vanilla in a shallow bowl.

Dip each slice of bread in milk mixture for a few seconds. Drain.

Melt margarine in a sprayed, large nonstick frying pan. Fry each piece of toast for 1 to 2 minutes until golden brown on bottom. Turn over with a spatula, and continue grilling until both sides are golden brown. This is best served hot.

....

Per Serving: Calories: 93.4; % of calories from fat: 18; Fat (gm): 1.9; Saturated Fat (gm): 0.4; Cholesterol (mg): 1.2; Sodium (mg): 180; Protein (gm): 5.6; Carbohydrate (gm): 13.4 Exchanges: Milk: 0.0; Vegetable: 0.0; Fruit: 0.0; Bread: 1.0; Meat: 0.0; Fat: 0.5

Rich and sweet, egg braid bread (challah) makes fabulous French toast.

THE BEST FRENCH TOAST WITH VERY BERRY SAUCE

MAKES 6 SERVINGS

> 1½ cups nonfat milk
> ½ cup egg substitute, or 2 eggs
> ½ teaspoon vanilla extract
> ½ teaspoon ground cinnamon
> 6 slices egg braid bread (challah), ½-inch thick
> 2 tablespoons reduced-fat margarine, or butter
> Butter-flavored cooking spray
> Very Berry Sauce (recipe follows)

Whisk together milk, egg substitute, vanilla, and cinnamon.

Dip bread in milk mixture for a few seconds. Drain.

Heat margarine in sprayed, large nonstick frying pan. Fry bread slices (in batches, if necessary) a few minutes until golden brown on bottom. Turn, using a spatula. Continue cooking until golden brown on both sides. Remove to individual serving dishes and serve with Very Berry Sauce.

....

COMPLETE RECIPE Per Serving: Calories: 164; % of calories from fat: 24; Fat (gm): 4.3; Saturated Fat (gm): 1.1; Cholesterol (mg): 21.6; Sodium (mg): 307; Protein (gm): 7.9; Carbohydrate (gm): 22.7 Exchanges: Milk: 0.0; Vegetable: 0.0; Fruit: 0.0; Bread: 1.5; Meat: 0.0; Fat: 1.0

*You can vary the berries in this depending on the season. For example, in the spring
you could use all strawberries; in August you could use all blueberries.*

VERY BERRY SAUCE

MAKES 2 CUPS (6 SERVINGS)

1 cup strawberries, stems removed and sliced

1 cup raspberries, washed and drained

1½ cups blueberries, washed and drained

¼ cup orange juice

Sugar-free sweetener, to taste

Combine strawberries, raspberries, and blueberries in saucepan. Mix in
orange juice and sweetener. Simmer for 10 minutes, stirring occasionally,
over medium heat. Continue cooking until berries are soft.

Cool before serving.

....

VERY BERRY SAUCE ONLY Per Serving: Calories: 44; % of calories from fat: 6; Fat (gm): 0.3;
Saturated Fat (gm): 0; Cholesterol (mg): 0; Sodium (mg): 1; Protein (gm): 0.7; Carbohydrate
(gm): 10.6 Exchanges: Milk: 0.0; Vegetable: 0.0; Fruit: 0.5; Bread: 0.0; Meat: 0.0; Fat: 0.0

Kids and grownups alike enjoy making their own waffles. You can keep waffles warm in a 200°F oven until ready to serve.

Buttermilk Waffles

MAKES 8 WAFFLES (1 PER SERVING)

1½ cups all-purpose flour

½ cup whole-wheat flour

2 tablespoons Splenda No Calorie Sweetener, or sugar

1 tablespoon baking powder

½ teaspoon baking soda

¾ cup reduced-fat buttermilk

⅓ cup canola oil blend

½ cup egg substitute, or 2 eggs

Butter-flavored cooking spray

Whisk together flours, sweetener, baking powder, baking soda, buttermilk, oil, and egg substitute in a large bowl just until smooth. Allow batter to stand for 15 minutes before using. Stir before using.

Heat a waffle-iron coated with cooking spray. Pour ¼ cup waffle mixture into center of waffle iron. Cook until brown, according to manufacturer's directions.

Serve with sugar-free maple syrup or Very Berry Sauce (see recipe on page 36). For Carnival Waffles, serve with 2 tablespoons fat-free whipped topping and sliced strawberries.

....

Per Serving: Calories: 208; % of calories from fat: 41; Fat (gm): 9.6; Saturated Fat (gm): 0.8; Cholesterol (mg): 0.9; Sodium (mg): 315; Protein (gm): 5.7; Carbohydrate (gm): 25.5 Exchanges: Milk: 0.0; Vegetable: 0.0; Fruit: 0.0; Bread: 1.5; Meat: 0.0; Fat: 2.0

Nutty Waffles

MAKES 8 (4-INCH) WAFFLES (1 PER SERVING)

1½ cups all-purpose flour
½ cup whole-wheat flour
2 tablespoons Splenda No Calorie Sweetener, or sugar
1 tablespoon baking powder
½ teaspoon baking soda
1¾ cups reduced-fat milk
⅓ cup canola oil blend
½ cup egg substitute, or 2 eggs
½ cup finely chopped pistachios, or nuts of choice
Butter-flavored cooking spray

In a bowl, whisk together flours, sweetener, baking powder, baking soda, milk, oil, eggs, and nuts. Let batter stand 15 minutes, then stir again.

Heat waffle-iron coated with cooking spray. Pour ¼ cup waffle batter into the center of waffle iron. Cook until brown, according to manufacturer's directions.

Serve hot with chopped fruit or sugar-free maple syrup.

....

Per Serving: Calories: 265; % of calories from fat: 46; Fat (gm): 13.9; Saturated Fat (gm): 1.9; Cholesterol (mg): 4.3; Sodium (mg): 372; Protein (gm): 8.4; Carbohydrate (gm): 28.1 Exchanges: Milk: 0.0; Vegetable: 0.0; Fruit: 0.0; Bread: 2.0; Meat: 0.0; Fat: 2.5

CREPES

MAKES 12 (6-INCH) CREPES (1 PER SERVING)

1½ cups sifted unbleached all-purpose flour

¾ cup egg substitute, or 3 eggs

2 cups nonfat milk

1 teaspoon Splenda No Calorie Sweetener, or 1 teaspoon sugar

Butter-flavored cooking spray

In a bowl, whisk together the flour, egg substitute, milk, and sweetener just until smooth.

Let batter stand for 15 to 20 minutes before cooking. When ready to cook crepes, pour about 2 tablespoons batter into a sprayed crepe pan or small nonstick skillet over medium heat. Swirl and tip the pan to coat the entire surface thinly. Fry crepe on one side only until set, about 1 minute. Spray pan between each crepe.

Place crepes briefly on regular or paper towels to absorb excess moisture, then stack cooked crepes between layers of waxed paper or aluminum foil. Use immediately.

To serve, spread 3 tablespoons of egg salad (see recipe on page 67) or tuna salad (see recipe on page 66) down the center of each crepe. Roll up crepes and serve.

....

Per Serving: Calories: 78; % of calories from fat: 2; Fat (gm): 0.2; Saturated Fat (gm): 0.1; Cholesterol (mg): 0.8; Sodium (mg): 46; Protein (gm): 4.5; Carbohydrate (gm): 14.2 Exchanges: Milk: 0.0; Vegetable: 0.0; Fruit: 0.0; Bread: 1.0; Meat: 0.0; Fat: 0.0

Scrambled eggs nest in a warm pita pocket to go, or enjoy them at the breakfast table.

BREAKFAST A-GO GO

MAKES 4 SERVINGS

1¼ cups egg substitute

¼ cup nonfat milk

Butter-flavored cooking spray

½ cup chopped ham (not canned)

Salt and pepper, to taste

2 whole-wheat pita pockets, cut in halves, warm

In a medium mixing bowl, using a whisk or fork, mix egg substitute and milk. Set aside.

Heat a sprayed frying pan over medium heat. Pour in eggs and ham. Cook, moving eggs around pan slowly with a spatula, lifting and stirring them until scrambled. Season with salt and pepper to taste.

Spoon eggs and ham into warm pita pickets. Serve warm.

....

Per Serving: Calories: 133; % of calories from fat: 13; Fat (gm): 2; Saturated Fat (gm): 0.5; Cholesterol (mg): 8.7; Sodium (mg): 493.7; Protein (gm): 13.9; Carbohydrate (gm): 16.6 Exchanges: Milk: 0.0; Vegetable: 0.0; Fruit: 0.0; Bread: 1.0; Meat: 2.0; Fat: 0.0

Peaches in Blankets

MAKES 6 SERVINGS

2 tablespoons reduced-fat margarine
Butter-flavored cooking spray
1 package (16 ounces) frozen peaches, defrosted
2 tablespoons cornstarch
2 tablespoons Splenda No Calorie Sweetener, or sugar
6 crepes (see recipe on page 39)

Melt margarine in a sprayed nonstick frying pan over medium heat. Fry peaches until tender, stirring often, about 4 to 5 minutes. Drain off juice to a small bowl and whisk in cornstarch and Splenda. Return mixture to peaches and warm again until sauce thickens slightly. Remove from heat.

Spread ¼ cup of peaches down center of crepe. Roll up crepe and set aside. Continue until all crepes have been filled.

Heat a sprayed, clean frying pan. Fry crepes, seam sides down, for a minute or two, only until heated.

Remove crepes to dessert plates, and divide up remaining peaches. Serve.

Per Serving: Calories: 134; % of calories from fat: 14; Fat (gm): 2.1; Saturated Fat (gm): 0.4; Cholesterol (mg): 0.8; Sodium (mg): 93; Protein (gm): 5.1; Carbohydrate (gm): 24.2 Exchanges: Milk: 0.0; Vegetable: 0.0; Fruit: 0.5; Bread: 1.0; Meat: 0.0; Fat: 0.5

Spud Pancakes with Sour Cream (For Teenagers)

MAKES 8 SERVINGS

4 medium potatoes, peeled and grated
½ cup grated onions
¼ cup egg substitute
Salt and pepper, to taste
2 tablespoons all-purpose flour
Butter-flavored cooking spray
1 cup nonfat, or reduced-fat, sour cream

Drain potatoes and press with paper towels to remove as much liquid as possible.

Using a large mixing bowl, stir together potatoes, onions, and egg substitute. Blend in salt, pepper, and flour.

Into a large heated and sprayed heavy frying pan, drop batter by heaping tablespoonfuls. Flatten with spatula to resemble pancakes. Cook over medium heat until golden brown on both sides. Turn, using a spatula, as necessary, until pancakes are cooked through.

Serve pancakes hot with sour cream.

....

Per Serving: Calories: 104; % of calories from fat: 1; Fat (gm): 0.1; Saturated Fat (gm): 0; Cholesterol (mg): 5; Sodium (mg): 43; Protein (gm): 4.2; Carbohydrate (gm): 21.2 Exchanges: Milk: 0.0; Vegetable: 0.0; Fruit: 0.0; Bread: 1.5; Meat: 0.0; Fat: 0.0

Crustless Carrot Quiche

MAKES 6 SERVINGS

> Butter-flavored cooking spray
> 2 cups shredded carrots
> 1¾ cups egg substitute, or 6 eggs
> 1¼ cups nonfat, or reduced-fat (2%) milk
> 1 tablespoon instant minced onions
> Salt and pepper, to taste
> ½ cup grated reduced-fat Cheddar cheese

Preheat oven to 350°F. Spray a 9-inch quiche, or nonstick baking, pan.

Using a small saucepan, add carrots and enough water to cover. Simmer about 5 minutes or until carrots are tender. Drain and set aside.

In a separate bowl, beat eggs with milk, onions, salt, and pepper. Stir in drained carrots and cheese.

Pour batter into prepared pan. Place pan in a larger pan and set in middle of oven. Using a pitcher, gently pour water into the larger pan until it reaches half-way up the sides of the quiche pan. Do not let water get into the quiche.

Bake for 35 minutes or until a knife inserted near the center comes out clean. Remove from oven and let stand for 5 minutes before serving.

....

Per Serving: Calories: 96; % of calories from fat: 20; Fat (gm): 2.1; Saturated Fat (gm): 1.2; Cholesterol (mg): 7.7; Sodium (mg): 264; Protein (gm): 11; Carbohydrate (gm): 8 Exchanges: Milk: 0.0; Vegetable: 2.0; Fruit: 0.0; Bread: 0.0; Meat: 1.0; Fat: 0.0

CHAPTER THREE

PIZZA, PASTA, AND GRAINS

For younger kids, use cookie cutters in their favorite shapes. You can use extra-large cutters to yield only one pizza per serving.

WHOLE-WHEAT PIZZA CUT-OUTS

MAKES 16 (2 ½-INCH) ROUNDS (2 PER SERVING)

1 package (1 pound) frozen whole-wheat pizza, or bread, dough, or Whole-Wheat Pizza Crust (recipe follows)
2 cups pizza sauce, or spaghetti sauce
½ cup grated reduced-fat mozzarella cheese
16 thin slices pepperoni

Preheat oven to 425°F. Use a nonstick cookie sheet.

Roll out dough on lightly floured cloth to a 12-inch circle. Using a 2½-inch cookie cutter or the rim of a drinking glass, cut out 16 rounds. Spread 2 tablespoons of sauce over each round. Sprinkle ½ tablespoon cheese on top of each round, and center a slice of pepperoni on top.

Place pizza rounds on cookie sheet. Bake on top rack of oven for 15 minutes or until crust is golden and topping is bubbly.

....

Per Serving: Calories: 218; % of calories from fat: 31; Fat (gm): 7.7; Saturated Fat (gm): 2.7; Cholesterol (mg): 16.7; Sodium (mg): 543; Protein (gm): 8.6; Carbohydrate (gm): 29.6 Exchanges: Milk: 0.0; Vegetable: 0.0; Fruit: 0.0; Bread: 2.0; Meat: 1.0; Fat: 0.5

Older children can help you stretch and toss the dough to make a crust. Just make sure they do the stretching and tossing over a clean table or counter.

WHOLE-WHEAT PIZZA CRUST

MAKES 1 (12-INCH) PIZZA CRUST (8 SERVINGS)

1 scant cup warm water, 105 to 115°

1 package (2¼ teaspoons) fast-rising active dry yeast

¾ cup whole-wheat flour

2 cups all-purpose flour

½ teaspoon salt

1 tablespoon olive oil

Olive oil-flavored cooking spray

Pour water into a measuring cup. Mix in yeast. Let mixture stand in warm area for 3 to 5 minutes, until yeast begins to bubble.

With electric mixer or food processor, mix together flours, salt, and oil. Mix in yeast and process just until a sticky, soft dough is formed, about 8 seconds in processor or 3 to 5 minutes with mixer.

Remove dough to lightly floured pastry cloth. Knead dough a few minutes until smooth. Set dough in bowl, and cover lightly with kitchen towel. Let dough rise 1 hour. Punch dough down, let stand 5 minutes, and roll and stretch out dough to a 12-inch round. Add topping and bake according to recipe directions.

....

Per Serving: Calories: 161; % of calories from fat: 12; Fat (gm): 2.2; Saturated Fat (gm): 0.3; Cholesterol (mg): 0; Sodium (mg): 148; Protein (gm): 4.9; Carbohydrate (gm): 30.5 Exchanges: Milk: 0.0; Vegetable: 0.0; Fruit: 0.0; Bread: 2.0; Meat: 0.0; Fat: 0.5

These pizzas are just adorable and taste good too. Surprise your children and their friends with this holiday treat.

Pizza Christmas Trees

MAKES 9 SERVINGS

1 package (1 pound) whole-wheat or plain frozen pizza dough, or
   homemade Whole-Wheat Pizza Crust (see recipe on page 47)
1 cup bottled pesto sauce

DECORATIONS FOR TREE:
   ½ cup frozen green peas, drained
   1 red bell pepper, cut into thin strips for garlands
   9 slices cooked carrot, for top of tree

Preheat oven to 400°F. Use a nonstick cookie sheet.

Roll out dough on a lightly floured surface to a rectangle about 12 inches long. Using a small, sharp knife, cut out 5-inch triangle shapes. Elongate dough and gently stretch, pulling out sides to make a tree shape.

Spread 1½ to 2 tablespoons pesto sauce over each tree. Using a spatula, carefully move trees to cookie sheet. Decorate trees with green peas for Christmas lights, red bell pepper strips for garlands, and a small round of carrot for the tree topper.

Bake 15 minutes or until crust is golden.

....

Per Serving: Calories: 145; % of calories from fat: 19; Fat (gm): 3.2; Saturated Fat (gm): 0.7; Cholesterol (mg): 1.1; Sodium (mg): 255; Protein (gm): 4.3; Carbohydrate (gm): 25.3 Exchanges: Milk: 0.0; Vegetable: 0.0; Fruit: 0.0; Bread: 1.5; Meat: 0.0; Fat: 0.5

Once an Italian specialty, pizza has become a cross-cultural dish in the United States. In all its forms, it's a tried-and-true children's favorite.

MEXICAN PIZZA

MAKES 1 (12-INCH) PIZZA (8 SERVINGS)

1 package whole-wheat or plain frozen pizza dough, or homemade Whole-Wheat Pizza Crust (see recipe on page 47)
Olive oil-flavored cooking spray
1 cup shredded reduced-fat mozzarella
16 cherry tomatoes, cut in half
1 cup chopped red bell peppers
½ cup thinly sliced onions, optional
1 tablespoon ground fajita spice

Preheat oven to 425°F. Use a 12-inch nonstick pizza pan.

Roll out dough on a lightly floured surface. Place dough in pan, stretching to cover bottom of pan. Spray dough. Sprinkle crust with cheese. Arrange tomatoes, peppers, and onions over crust. Sprinkle with fajita spice.

Bake pizza on top rack of oven for 15 to 20 minutes or just until crust is golden.

....

Per Serving: Calories: 131; % of calories from fat: 22; Fat (gm): 3.2; Saturated Fat (gm): 1.3; Cholesterol (mg): 7.5; Sodium (mg): 415; Protein (gm): 5.8; Carbohydrate (gm): 20.2 Exchanges: Milk: 0.0; Vegetable: 1.0; Fruit: 0.0; Bread: 1.0; Meat: 0.0; Fat: 0.5

For a main course, add 1 cup minced cooked chicken and ½ cup chopped red bell pepper.

MOLDED ANGEL HAIR PASTA

MAKES 6 SERVINGS

>½ pound angel hair pasta, cooked according to package directions
>½ cup minced green onion
>3 tablespoons reduced-fat margarine
>½ cup grated carrots
>Butter-flavored cooking spray

Drain pasta and stir in green onions, margarine, and carrots.

Spray 6 (6-ounce) ramekins or 1 medium-size mixing bowl with cooking spray. Divide pasta and pat into ramekins, packing lightly, or pack the pasta into one mixing bowl. Chill 15 minutes and unmold onto separate plates or a serving platter. Surround with cut vegetables, celery sticks, sliced cucumbers, and cherry tomatoes (not included in nutritional data).

....

Per Serving: Calories: 172; % of calories from fat: 19; Fat (gm): 3.5; Saturated Fat (gm): 0.6; Cholesterol (mg): 0; Sodium (mg): 77; Protein (gm): 4.9; Carbohydrate (gm): 29.6 Exchanges: Milk: 0.0; Vegetable: 0.0; Fruit: 0.0; Bread: 2.0; Meat: 0.0; Fat: 0.5

Grits separate true Southerners from Yankees. Like pasta or rice, they serve as a base for just about anything you like.

TRUE GRITS

MAKES 6 SERVINGS

3 cups cold water
Salt and pepper, to taste
2 bay leaves
1 teaspoon minced garlic
¾ cup quick-cooking white hominy grits
2 tablespoons reduced-fat margarine, or butter, optional

Pour water into a saucepan. Add salt, pepper, bay leaves, and garlic. Bring water to a full boil over medium-high heat. Whisk in grits, slowly. Continue whisking 3 to 4 minutes. Turn off heat and let grits stand, covered, for 5 to 6 minutes. Discard bay leaves. Stir in margarine (if using) until it melts.

....

Per Serving: Calories: 78; % of calories from fat: 23; Fat (gm): 2.1; Saturated Fat (gm): 0.4; Cholesterol (mg): 0; Sodium (mg): 46; Protein (gm): 1.6; Carbohydrate (gm): 14.8 Exchanges: Milk: 0.0; Vegetable: 0.0; Fruit: 0.0; Bread: 1.0; Meat: 0.0; Fat: 0.5

Orzo, rice-shaped pasta, is the ideal size for a salad. This dish would also taste fine made with brown rice.

ORZO SALAD

MAKES 8 SERVINGS (1 CUP PER SERVING)

4 cups cooked orzo, preferably whole-wheat

½ cup grated reduced-fat Cheddar cheese, or crumbled feta cheese

¼ cup sliced black olives

¾ cup chopped parsley

1 cup cherry tomatoes, cut in halves

2 cups rinsed, trimmed baby spinach

DRESSING:

1 tablespoon olive oil

¼ cup cider vinegar

Salt and pepper, to taste

Chopped fresh cilantro, optional

In a deep serving bowl, combine the orzo with the cheese, olives, parsley, tomatoes, and spinach and toss. Mix together dressing ingredients, sprinkle over salad, and toss again.

Serve at room temperature or chilled.

Per Serving: Calories: 173; % of calories from fat: 29; Fat (gm): 5.7; Saturated Fat (gm): 2.1; Cholesterol (mg): 10; Sodium (mg): 172; Protein (gm): 7.7; Carbohydrate (gm): 23.6 Exchanges: Milk: 0.0; Vegetable: 0.0; Fruit: 0.0; Bread: 1.5; Meat: 0.5; Fat: 1.0

Use very ripe plum tomatoes and fresh basil for best results. To peel tomatoes, carefully put them in a bowl of very hot water. Let stand for 5 minutes, then drain. For older children, you can add a 10-ounce package of frozen artichoke hearts, cooked according to package directions.

ZITI WITH FRESH TOMATO SAUCE

MAKES 8 SERVINGS (½ CUP PER SERVING)

2 tablespoons balsamic vinegar

2 tablespoons olive oil

Salt and pepper, to taste

1½ pounds ripe plum tomatoes, peeled, seeded, and coarsely chopped

½ cup torn fresh basil leaves

3 cups cooked ziti

In a bowl, whisk together the vinegar, oil, salt, and pepper. Mix in tomatoes and basil.

Place hot, drained ziti in a large bowl, and stir in sauce. Serve.

....

Per Serving: Calories: 172; % of calories from fat: 22; Fat (gm): 4.2; Saturated Fat (gm): 0.6; Cholesterol (mg): 0; Sodium (mg): 10; Protein (gm): 4.9; Carbohydrate (gm): 29 Exchanges: Milk: 0.0; Vegetable: 0.0; Fruit: 0.0; Bread: 2.0; Meat: 0.0; Fat: 1.0

Serve this for lunch, or tote it to the next family picnic.

ELBOW MACARONI SALAD

MAKES 6 SERVINGS

3 cups cooked, drained whole-wheat elbow macaroni
1 cup defrosted frozen corn kernels
1 cup chopped tomatoes
1 cup defrosted frozen peas
⅓ cup rice vinegar

Place macaroni in a salad bowl. Toss with corn, tomatoes, and peas. Mix in rice vinegar. Serve at room temperature or cold.

Per Serving: Calories: 141; % of calories from fat: 4; Fat (gm): 0.7; Saturated Fat (gm): 0.1; Cholesterol (mg): 0; Sodium (mg): 24; Protein (gm): 6.1; Carbohydrate (gm): 29.2 Exchanges: Milk: 0.0; Vegetable: 0.0; Fruit: 0.0; Bread: 2.0; Meat: 0.0; Fat: 0.0

It is a good idea to squeeze-dry defrosted spinach with paper towels. You can always top the pasta with a sprinkle of grated cheese.

ZINGY MARINARA SAUCE ON A BED OF NOODLES

MAKES 6 SERVINGS

8 ounces whole-wheat pasta

1 package (10 ounces) frozen chopped spinach, defrosted, well drained

½ cup grated carrots

2 cups Marinara Sauce (recipe follows)

Bring a pot of salted water to a boil over medium-high heat. Add pasta and cook according to package directions or until pasta is just tender. Drain.

Put pasta in a large bowl. Toss pasta with spinach, carrots, and Marinara Sauce.

Divide pasta onto individual plates and serve.

....

COMPLETE RECIPE Per Serving: Calories: 188; % of calories from fat: 4; Fat (gm): 0.8; Saturated Fat (gm): 0.2; Cholesterol (mg): 0; Sodium (mg): 389; Protein (gm): 8.5; Carbohydrate (gm): 39.8 Exchanges: Milk: 0.0; Vegetable: 0.0; Fruit: 0.0; Bread: 0.0; Meat: 0.0; Fat: 0.0

Marinara Sauce

MAKES 2¾ TO 3 CUPS (¼ CUP PER SERVING)

Olive oil-flavored cooking spray
½ cup chopped onion
2 cloves garlic, minced
½ cup grated carrots
½ cup chopped green bell pepper
1 can (6 ounces) tomato paste
1 can (8 ounces) tomato sauce
1 cup chopped fresh tomato
1½ cups water
1½ teaspoons oregano
½ teaspoon basil
Salt and pepper, to taste

In a sprayed saucepan, sauté onions, garlic, carrots, and green pepper. Continue cooking for about 5 minutes, covered, stirring occasionally so vegetables do not stick to pan.

Mix in tomato paste, tomato sauce, tomatoes, and water. Blend in oregano, basil, salt, and pepper.

Cover and simmer for 4 to 5 minutes. Stir occasionally.

....

MARINARA SAUCE ONLY Per Serving: Calories: 30; % of calories from fat: 5; Fat (gm): 0.2; Saturated Fat (gm): 0.1; Cholesterol (mg): 0; Sodium (mg): 235; Protein (gm): 1.3; Carbohydrate (gm): 7 Exchanges: Milk: 0.0; Vegetable: 1.0; Fruit: 0.0; Bread: 0.0; Meat: 0.0; Fat: 0.0

You can substitute mushrooms sautéed in a sprayed nonstick pan for the peppers. Or add ½ cup chopped green onions for flavor.

PINENUTTY THAI PASTA (FOR TEENAGERS)

MAKES 6 SERVINGS

8 ounces whole-wheat, or spinach, noodles
½ cup pine nuts, or walnuts
½ cup reduced-fat ricotta cheese
1 cup red bell pepper strips
1 cup chopped tomatoes

Bring a pot of salted water to a boil over medium-high heat. Cook pasta according to package directions or until al dente, tender but not mushy. Drain.

Put noodles in a large bowl. Toss with pine nuts, cheese, pepper strips, and tomatoes.

Per Serving: Calories: 249; % of calories from fat: 34; Fat (gm): 10.1; Saturated Fat (gm): 1.7; Cholesterol (mg): 6.4; Sodium (mg): 29; Protein (gm): 9.9; Carbohydrate (gm): 33.6 Exchanges: Milk: 0.0; Vegetable: 0.0; Fruit: 0.0; Bread: 2.0; Meat: 0.0; Fat: 2.0

CHAPTER FOUR

SANDWICHES AND SALADS

For older children you might want to layer thin slices of red onion on the sandwich with the tomato slices.

GRILLED CHEESE SANDWICH

MAKES 2 SERVINGS (½ SANDWICH PER SERVING)

1 slice reduced-fat Swiss cheese
2 slices whole-wheat bread
2 slices tomato
Butter-flavored cooking spray

Arrange cheese over one slice of bread. Set tomato slices over cheese and cover with remaining slice of bread.

Heat a sprayed nonstick frying pan over medium heat. Fry sandwich 1 minute or just until golden on bottom. Using a spatula, turn sandwich over and continue cooking until golden on both sides, another 1 to 2 minutes. Remove to a plate and cut sandwich in half or quarters.

....

Per Serving: Calories: 120; % of calories from fat: 34; Fat (gm): 4.6; Saturated Fat (gm): 2.5; Cholesterol (mg): 12.5; Sodium (mg): 170; Protein (gm): 7.6; Carbohydrate (gm): 12.3 Exchanges: Milk: 0.0; Vegetable: 0.0; Fruit: 0.0; Bread: 1.0; Meat: 0.5; Fat: 0.5

Children of all ages enjoy Mexican-style dishes. This is no exception. Sprinkle each tortilla with extra cheese and/or salsa if desired. This is good for breakfast, lunch, or a light dinner.

Southwest Scrambled Egg Tortilla Wrap

MAKES 4 SERVINGS

Olive oil-flavored cooking spray
1 cup egg substitute, or 4 eggs
½ teaspoon chili powder
4 8-inch whole-wheat tortillas, warmed
½ cup shredded reduced-fat mozzarella cheese
⅓ cup salsa

Heat a large, sprayed nonstick frying pan over medium heat. Add egg substitute and cook, stirring, until scrambled. Sprinkle with chili powder.

Arrange and divide eggs evenly on the whole-wheat tortillas. Sprinkle with cheese and salsa. Roll up tortilla.

Arrange a tortilla on each plate.

....

Per Serving: Calories: 184; % of calories from fat: 25; Fat (gm): 4.9; Saturated Fat (gm): 1.3; Cholesterol (mg): 7.5; Sodium (mg): 575; Protein (gm): 12.5; Carbohydrate (gm): 20.2 Exchanges: Milk: 0.0; Vegetable: 0.0; Fruit: 0.0; Bread: 1.0; Meat: 1.0; Fat: 1.0

*Serve fajita in a warm whole-flour tortilla or in a whole-wheat pita half over a
bed of chopped lettuce. If you like, you can sprinkle fajitas with chopped cilantro.*

CHICKEN FAJITAS

MAKES 4 TO 6 SERVINGS

2 tablespoons canola oil

Olive oil-flavored cooking spray

¾ cup sliced onion

1½ cups sliced red, or green, bell peppers

½ teaspoon garlic powder

2 whole skinless, boneless chicken breasts, cut into ½-inch strips

1 tablespoon fajitas spice mix

Heat oil in a sprayed nonstick frying pan. Add onion, peppers, and garlic
powder, and cook over medium heat, stirring occasionally, about 5 minutes
or until the onions and peppers are tender.

Add chicken and continue cooking, stirring occasionally, until chicken is
cooked through. Season with fajitas spice. Serve hot in a tortilla wrap or pita
pocket (not included in nutritionals).

....

Per Serving: Calories: 223; % of calories from fat: 34; Fat (gm): 8.4; Saturated Fat (gm): 0.9;
Cholesterol (mg): 68.4; Sodium (mg): 213; Protein (gm): 28.1; Carbohydrate (gm): 7.8
Exchanges: Milk: 0.0; Vegetable: 1.0; Fruit: 0.0; Bread: 0.0; Meat: 4.0; Fat: 0.0

Quesadillas consist of a fried tortilla filled with shrimp, cheese, or other foods. Grilled lightly on both sides, it is a tasty finger food. To use as an appetizer, cut into wedges and serve with salsa. A great variation of this recipe is to substitute a piece of pan-fried fish for the shrimp.

One interesting thing about tortillas is that they now come in various flavors. You can choose spinach, tomato, white (flour), or whole-wheat tortillas.

SHRIMP QUESADILLAS

MAKES 6 SERVINGS

Butter-flavored cooking spray
18 extra-large shrimp, peeled, deveined, tail discarded
Fajitas spice, to taste
6 (6-inch) whole-wheat, or flour, tortillas
6 small romaine lettuce leaves
12 (½-inch thick) slices tomato
Salsa, optional

Heat a sprayed nonstick frying pan over medium heat. Add shrimp and pan fry for 1 minute. Turn the shrimp, spraying the pan again if necessary, and cook until opaque and cooked through, about 1 minute. Sprinkle shrimp with fajitas spice.

Arrange a lettuce leaf, 2 tomato slices, and 3 shrimp on half of each tortilla. Fold the other half over the filling, pressing the tortilla edges together.

Heat a sprayed nonstick frying pan over medium heat. Add the quesadillas and fry 1 to 2 minutes or until lightly toasted on the bottom; then turn and fry the other side for 1 to 2 minutes or until golden.

Serve warm, with salsa if desired.

....

Per Serving: Calories: 151; % of calories from fat: 21; Fat (gm): 3.5; Saturated Fat (gm): 0.1; Cholesterol (mg): 31.9; Sodium (mg): 344; Protein (gm): 8.7; Carbohydrate (gm): 20.1 Exchanges: Milk: 0.0; Vegetable: 1.0; Fruit: 0.0; Bread: 1.0; Meat: 1.0; Fat: 0.0

This is a fine way to use up leftover turkey after Thanksgiving. Top the quesadillas with a tablespoon of stuffing if you have any. The rest of the year, you can use deli turkey breast to make this quick, light lunch or after-school snack. Older kids can make quesadillas themselves.

TURKEY QUESADILLAS

MAKES 4 SERVINGS

1 cup chopped white turkey meat
½ cup chopped green onions
¼ cup nonfat sour cream, or yogurt
4 (6-inch) whole-wheat tortillas
Butter-flavored cooking spray
Salsa, optional

In a bowl, toss turkey with onions and sour cream.

Place each tortilla on a plate, and spread filling over half of each. Fold tortillas in half, pressing edges together.

Heat a sprayed, large nonstick frying pan over medium heat. Add the quesadillas and fry 1 to 2 minutes or until lightly toasted on the bottom. Then turn and fry the other side for 1 to 2 minutes or until golden.

Serve warm, with salsa if desired.

....

Per Serving: Calories: 196; % of calories from fat: 16; Fat (gm): 3.3; Saturated Fat (gm): 0.1; Cholesterol (mg): 37.8; Sodium (mg): 347; Protein (gm): 18; Carbohydrate (gm): 21.4 Exchanges: Milk: 0.0; Vegetable: 0.0; Fruit: 0.0; Bread: 1.0; Meat: 2.0; Fat: 0.0

Sloppy Joes, seasoned ground beef piled into sandwiches, have been a favorite on the American table for decades.

GOOEY SLOPPY JOES

MAKES 6 SERVINGS

1 pound lean ground turkey, or beef

½ cup chopped onion

½ cup chopped green, or red, bell pepper

1 can (8 ounces) tomato sauce

¼ cup catsup

1 teaspoon Worcestershire sauce

½ teaspoon chili powder

½ teaspoon pepper

½ teaspoon garlic powder

3 whole-wheat sandwich rolls, or hamburger buns, cut in half, warmed

Cook ground turkey, onion, and pepper in nonstick frying pan over medium heat, stirring occasionally, until turkey is browned. Drain. Return to the pan.

Stir in tomato sauce, catsup, Worcestershire sauce, chili powder, pepper, and garlic powder. Simmer for 10 minutes, stirring often. Taste and adjust seasonings if desired.

Set bottom half of each roll on a plate. Spoon Sloppy Joe mixture over roll, then top with other half of roll. Serve. These sandwiches are good with coleslaw.

....

Per Serving: Calories: 151; % of calories from fat: 11; Fat (gm): 1.9; Saturated Fat (gm): 0; Cholesterol (mg): 30; Sodium (mg): 437; Protein (gm): 20; Carbohydrate (gm): 15 Exchanges: Milk: 0.0; Vegetable: 0.0; Fruit: 0.0; Bread: 1.0; Meat: 2.0; Fat: 0.0

These sandwiches are also great with cooked salmon or lobster, if you're lucky enough to have some on hand. Cut the servings in half for small children.

ROCKY SHORE TUNA ROLL

MAKES 6 SERVINGS

> 2 cans (3½ ounces each) tuna, packed in water
> 1 cup finely chopped celery
> ½ cup minced onion, or finely chopped red bell pepper
> ½ cup reduced-fat, or fat-free, mayonnaise
> Salt and pepper, to taste
> Butter-flavored cooking spray
> 2 tablespoons reduced-fat margarine, or butter
> 6 hot dog rolls, split

Drain and flake tuna into a bowl. Stir in celery, onion, and mayonnaise. Mix well. Season with salt and pepper.

Spray nonstick skillet and melt margarine. Toast hot dog roll halves, cut side down, until just golden, about 1 minute.

Remove rolls from pan. Fill each roll with tuna salad. Best served warm.

....

Per Serving: Calories: 245; % of calories from fat: 38; Fat (gm): 10.1; Saturated Fat (gm): 1.8; Cholesterol (mg): 16.4; Sodium (mg): 527; Protein (gm): 12.9; Carbohydrate (gm): 24.8 Exchanges: Milk: 0.0; Vegetable: 0.0; Fruit: 0.0; Bread: 2.0; Meat: 1.0; Fat: 1.0

Egg salad can be served plain on some lettuce leaves with a couple of slices of tomato, but if you have a neighborhood bakery, check and see if you can buy a horn-of-plenty-shaped roll. It's worth the effort; children will find it delightful.

Egg Salad Stuffed in a Horn

MAKES 8 SERVINGS (½ HORN PER SERVING)

4 (6-inch) horn rolls
16 hard-boiled egg whites, chopped
¾ cup chopped red bell pepper
½ cup chopped onion, optional
¼ cup reduced-fat, or fat-free, mayonnaise
Salt and white pepper, to taste

Cut the rolls in half lengthwise, and scoop out the fluffy insides, leaving the shell.

Place egg whites in a bowl. Add bell pepper, onion, and mayonnaise. Season with salt and white pepper. Mix well. Lightly fill horn halves with egg salad.

If you like, lightly warm filled horns in a 325°F oven for 5 minutes before serving.

Per Serving: Calories: 169; % of calories from fat: 25; Fat (gm): 4.7; Saturated Fat (gm): 0.9; Cholesterol (mg): 19.9; Sodium (mg): 357; Protein (gm): 10.8; Carbohydrate (gm): 20.1 Exchanges: Milk: 0.0; Vegetable: 0.0; Fruit: 0.0; Bread: 1.5; Meat: 1.0; Fat: 1.0

Garbage Salad is called that because it's a simple toss of whatever salad ingredients you happen to have on hand.

GARBAGE SALAD

MAKES 4 TO 5 SERVINGS (1 ½ TO 2 CUPS PER SERVING)

> 6 cups shredded lettuce
> ½ cup sliced tomatoes
> ½ cup sliced cucumbers
> ½ cup frozen peas, cooked, drained
> ½ cup frozen corn, cooked, drained
> ¼ cup sliced black olives
> Yogurt Herb Dressing (recipe follows)

Using a large salad bowl, toss lettuce together with tomatoes, cucumbers, peas, corn, and olives. Add dressing (recipe follows) and toss salad again. Spoon onto individual plates and serve.

YOGURT HERB DRESSING

MAKES 1 ¼ CUPS (4 TO 5 SERVINGS)

> 1 cup plain fat-free yogurt
> ¼ cup finely chopped onion
> ¼ cup trimmed fresh dillweed
> ¼ cup fresh parsley leaves
> Salt, pepper, and garlic powder, to taste

Using a food processor, pulse the yogurt, onion, dill, parsley, salt, pepper, and garlic powder until smooth. Place in a covered container and chill until ready to serve.

....

Per Serving: Calories: 89; % of calories from fat: 5; Fat (gm): 0.5; Saturated Fat (gm): 0.1; Cholesterol (mg): 1.2; Sodium (mg): 74; Protein (gm): 6.2; Carbohydrate (gm): 16.4 Exchanges: Milk: 0.0; Vegetable: 3.0; Fruit: 0.0; Bread: 0.0; Meat: 0.0; Fat: 0.0

Serve this hearty salad as is or with fat-free sour cream, guacamole, and/or a few fat-free nacho chips.

Taco Salad

MAKES 4 TO 6 SERVINGS

8 cups shredded head lettuce
Olive oil-flavored cooking spray
¾ pound 90% lean ground beef
½ teaspoon garlic powder
2 teaspoons chili powder
1½ cups chopped fresh tomatoes
½ cup shredded reduced-fat Cheddar cheese
1½ cups chopped red onion

Place lettuce in a large salad bowl. Set aside.

Heat a sprayed nonstick frying pan over medium heat. Add beef and cook, stirring occasionally, until all traces of pink are gone. Season with garlic powder and chili powder. Sprinkle ground beef over lettuce. Spoon tomatoes over and around beef. Sprinkle with cheese and onions.

Bring salad to the table, toss, and divide onto individual plates.

. . . .

Per Serving: Calories: 252; % of calories from fat: 47; Fat (gm): 13.5; Saturated Fat (gm): 5.7; Cholesterol (mg): 59.1; Sodium (mg): 195; Protein (gm): 22; Carbohydrate (gm): 11.7 Exchanges: Milk: 0.0; Vegetable: 2.0; Fruit: 0.0; Bread: 0.0; Meat: 3.0; Fat: 1.0

Blueberries are a good source of vitamin C and manganese. And although the science is still preliminary, they seem to be good at helping to control blood sugar.

BLUEBERRY SALAD

MAKES 4 SERVINGS (2 CUPS PER SERVING)

>   6 cups assorted spring greens, washed and dried on paper towels
>
>   2 cups fresh blueberries, rinsed and drained on paper towels
>
>   ½ cup pine nuts, or chopped walnuts
>
>   Salt and pepper, to taste
>
>   Green Dressing (recipe follows)

In a salad bowl, toss greens, blueberries, and pine nuts. Sprinkle with salt and pepper to taste. When ready to serve, toss salad with Green Dressing (recipe follows). Divide salad onto individual serving bowls or plates.

....

COMPLETE RECIPE Per Serving: Calories: 167; % of calories from fat: 61; Fat (gm): 12; Saturated Fat (gm): 0.9; Cholesterol (mg): 0; Sodium (mg): 9; Protein (gm): 3.4; Carbohydrate (gm): 14.2
Exchanges: Milk: 0.0; Vegetable: 0.0; Fruit: 1.0; Bread: 0.0; Meat: 0.0; Fat: 2.0

GREEN DRESSING

MAKES 4 SERVINGS (ABOUT 2 CUPS TOTAL)

  1 cup plain fat-free yogurt
  2 tablespoons balsamic vinegar
  ½ cup minced chives
  ½ cup minced parsley, or cilantro

In a small bowl, combine yogurt with vinegar, chives, and parsley or cilantro. Place in a covered container and refrigerate until serving time.

....

GREEN DRESSING ONLY Per Serving: Calories: 16; % of calories from fat: 4; Fat (gm): 0.1; Saturated Fat (gm): 0.1; Cholesterol (mg): 0.5; Sodium (mg): 20; Protein (gm): 1.5; Carbohydrate (gm): 2.4 Exchanges: Milk: 0.0; Vegetable: 0.0; Fruit: 0.0; Bread: 0.0; Meat: 0.0; Fat: 0.0

Sprinkle salad with sesame seeds for a crunchy taste.

Far East Salad in Radicchio Cups

MAKES 6 SERVINGS

1 can (15 ounces) chick peas, drained and rinsed

1½ cups bean sprouts, washed and drained

1 cup chopped tomato

½ cup chopped green onion, optional

½ pound firm tofu, cut into ½-inch cubes

¼ cup rice vinegar

6 radicchio leaves

In a salad bowl, toss together the chick peas, bean sprouts, tomatoes, onions, and tofu. Pour vinegar over salad and toss ingredients together.

Arrange mixture on radicchio leaves to serve.

....

Per Serving: Calories: 133; % of calories from fat: 17; Fat (gm): 2.5; Saturated Fat (gm): 0.4; Cholesterol (mg): 0; Sodium (mg): 223; Protein (gm): 7.9; Carbohydrate (gm): 20.7 Exchanges: Milk: 0.0; Vegetable: 0.0; Fruit: 0.0; Bread: 1.0; Meat: 1.0; Fat: 0.0

A good idea for a special summer lunch, especially appealing to teenagers. Use a grill screen to prevent fruit from falling into grill. Leave off dressing for younger children. For older children serve fruit on a lettuce leaf.

GRILLED FRUIT SALAD WITH PINEAPPLE CHUTNEY

MAKES 8 SERVINGS

½ cup Pineapple Chutney (recipe follows)
1 cup plain reduced-fat yogurt
1 8-ounce bag salad mix
1 small cantaloupe, peeled, seeded, cut into 1-inch wedges
1 peeled, cored, and sliced pineapple, drained
1 banana, peeled, cut into 8 pieces
Butter-flavored cooking spray

In a small bowl, stir together the Pineapple Chutney with the yogurt. Cover and refrigerate until needed. Stir before serving.

Preheat grill according to manufacturer's directions, or use a stove top grill. Spray fruits with cooking spray. Grill cantaloupe wedges and pineapple slices about 1 to 3 minutes, turning as needed until lightly golden. Arrange on salad plates. Grill banana 1 to 2 minutes, turning as needed, until lightly golden. Transfer to salad plates.

Spoon chutney over salads and serve immediately.

....

COMPLETE RECIPE Per Serving: Calories: 112; % of calories from fat: 6; Fat (gm): 0.8; Saturated Fat (gm): 0.4; Cholesterol (mg): 1.8; Sodium (mg): 39; Protein (gm): 3.1; Carbohydrate (gm): 24.7 Exchanges: Milk: 0.0; Vegetable: 0.0; Fruit: 2.0; Bread: 0.0; Meat: 0.0; Fat: 0.0

Homemade fruit chutney can be bottled to make a nice gift.

PINEAPPLE CHUTNEY (FOR TEENAGERS)

MAKES ABOUT 2 CUPS (1 TABLESPOON PER SERVING)

2 cans (8 ounces each) crushed pineapple, packed in fruit juice, well
  drained

½ cup white vinegar

½ cup brown sugar, or Splenda No Calorie Sweetener

½ cup chopped onion

1 teaspoon minced ginger

¼ cup golden raisins

½ teaspoon minced garlic

1 teaspoon ground cinnamon

½ teaspoon ground cloves

Using a large saucepan, combine all ingredients. Bring mixture to a boil, and
reduce heat to medium. Continue cooking about 5 minutes until mixture
thickens slightly. Stir occasionally. Reduce heat to simmer and cook, stirring
occasionally, until mixture is thick, about 10 minutes longer. Let cool. Taste
and adjust seasonings as necessary.

Spoon chutney into clean glass jars and refrigerate until needed. Stir before
serving.

....

PINEAPPLE CHUTNEY ONLY Per Serving: Calories: 21; % of calories from fat: 1; Fat (gm): 0;
Saturated Fat (gm): 0; Cholesterol (mg): 0; Sodium (mg): 0.5; Protein (gm): 0.1; Carbohydrate
(gm): 5.1 Exchanges: Milk: 0.0; Vegetable: 0.0; Fruit: 0.0; Bread: 0.0; Meat: 0.0; Fat: 0.0

To trim asparagus, simply discard the woody ends of each stalk.

WHITE AND GREEN POTATO SALAD

MAKES 6 SERVINGS

2 cups cut-up (1-inch pieces) trimmed asparagus
1 pound unpeeled small new potatoes
2 tablespoons reduced-fat mayonnaise, or reduced-fat salad
    dressing
Salt and pepper, to taste

Bring a pan of salted water to a boil. Add asparagus and cook for 3 to 4
minutes. Drain asparagus and rinse under cold running water; drain on
paper toweling. Reserve cooking water.

Bring water to a boil, add potatoes, and cook until fork tender, about 10
minutes, depending on size of potatoes. Drain.

In a salad bowl, gently mix the asparagus and potatoes together. Toss with
mayonnaise or salad dressing. Sprinkle with salt and pepper to taste. For
older children, sprinkle with chopped parsley or cilantro if desired.

....

Per Serving: Calories: 94; % of calories from fat: 16; Fat (gm): 1.7; Saturated Fat (gm): 0.3;
Cholesterol (mg): 1.6; Sodium (mg): 48; Protein (gm): 2.9; Carbohydrate (gm): 18 Exchanges:
Milk: 0.0; Vegetable: 0.0; Fruit: 0.0; Bread: 1.0; Meat: 0.0; Fat: 0.5

When serving peanuts, always make sure that no one is allergic to them. For those who like spice, you can add ¼ teaspoon crushed red pepper.

Thai Salad (For Teenagers)

MAKES 6 SERVINGS

> 10 ounces cellophane noodles, available at large supermarkets and Asian food stores
> ½ cup unsalted peanuts
> 1 teaspoon grated ginger
> ¼ cup chopped fresh cilantro, or basil
> ½ cup lime juice
> ½ cup reduced-sodium soy sauce
> 3 tablespoons Splenda No calorie Sweetener

In a large bowl, cover cellophane noodles with hot water. Drain noodles. Using kitchen scissors, cut the softened noodles into 2- to 3- inch pieces. Noodles will be soft and clear in color. Cool. Place noodles in a salad bowl.

Using a food processor, chop peanuts with ginger. Toss peanut mixture with noodles, then toss noodles with cilantro.

In a small bowl, combine lime juice, soy sauce, and Splenda. Stir mixture evenly into noodle salad. Serve at room temperature.

Per Serving: Calories: 262; % of calories from fat: 20; Fat (gm): 6.1; Saturated Fat (gm): 0.8; Cholesterol (mg): 0; Sodium (mg): 679; Protein (gm): 5; Carbohydrate (gm): 48.7 Exchanges: Milk: 0.0; Vegetable: 0.0; Fruit: 0.0; Bread: 3.0; Meat: 0.0; Fat: 1.0

CHAPTER FIVE

SIDES AND SOUPS

Children who wouldn't dream of eating cabbage in any other form will often eat coleslaw. A good thing, too, since cabbage is loaded with vitamin C and other healthy vitamins and minerals.

NUTTY COLESLAW

MAKES 12 SERVINGS (½ CUP PER SERVING)

4 cups shredded green cabbage

2 cups shredded red cabbage

¼ cup chopped walnuts, or almonds

¼ cup chopped pecans

½ cup grated carrots

DRESSING:

¾ cup fat-free mayonnaise

¼ cup red wine vinegar

3 tablespoons Splenda No Calorie Sweetener, or sugar

Salt and pepper, to taste

Toss together green and red cabbage in a mixing bowl. Mix in walnuts, pecans, and carrots.

Mix together the mayonnaise, vinegar, sweetener, salt, and pepper in a small bowl. Mix the dressing into the salad.

Serve immediately or cover with plastic wrap and refrigerate until ready to serve. Toss the coleslaw before serving.

Per Serving: Calories: 53; % of calories from fat: 52; Fat (gm): 3.3; Saturated Fat (gm): 0.3; Cholesterol (mg): 0; Sodium (mg): 131; Protein (gm): 1.1; Carbohydrate (gm): 5.7 Exchanges: Milk: 0.0; Vegetable: 1.0; Fruit: 0.0; Bread: 0.0; Meat: 0.0; Fat: 0.5

To turn this recipe into a lunch dish, just omit the raisins and add 4 cups of sliced sautéed mushrooms and/or a little chopped turkey or chicken. Keep any extra cooked noodles in a self-sealing bag in the refrigerator for a few days. For easy meals, use the cooked noodles as a base for many dishes, or just reheat them with a little reduced-fat margarine or butter.

STIR-FRIED NOODLE PUDDING

MAKES 8 TO 10 SERVINGS

    2 tablespoons reduced-fat margarine, or butter
    6 cups egg noodles, cooked according to package directions,
        drained and cooled
    1 cup 1% low-fat cottage cheese
    ¾ cup reduced-fat sour cream
    ¼ cup raisins

Using a nonstick frying pan, melt the margarine. Add the noodles, stirring to coat them with margarine. Stir in cottage cheese, sour cream, and raisins. Heat and serve.

....

Per Serving: Calories: 185; % of calories from fat: 27; Fat (gm): 5.6; Saturated Fat (gm): 2.4; Cholesterol (mg): 37; Sodium (mg): 162; Protein (gm): 8.3; Carbohydrate (gm): 25.6 Exchanges: Milk: 0.0; Vegetable: 0.0; Fruit: 0.0; Bread: 2.0; Meat: 0.0; Fat: 1.0

Corn is a good source of thiamin, potassium, and some iron. It's often the only vegetable some kids will eat.

TOSSED CORN OFF THE COB

MAKES 6 SERVINGS

4 ears corn, cooked, or 3 cups cooked corn kernels, drained

1 cup chopped tomatoes

1 cup chopped green, or red, bell pepper

1 tablespoon bacon bits

½ teaspoon taco spice

Salt and pepper, to taste

If using whole ears of corn, stand corn on end and carefully scrape off kernels with a small, sharp knife. Put corn in a mixing bowl. Add tomatoes, peppers, bacon bits, and taco spice. Season with salt and pepper.

Cover and refrigerate until serving time. Toss again before serving, and adjust seasonings if desired.

....

Per Serving: Calories: 54; % of calories from fat: 10; Fat (gm): 0.7; Saturated Fat (gm): 0.2; Cholesterol (mg): 0.8; Sodium (mg): 53; Protein (gm): 2.3; Carbohydrate (gm): 12 Exchanges: Milk: 0.0; Vegetable: 0.0; Fruit: 0.0; Bread: 1.0; Meat: 0.0; Fat: 0.0

Sweet potatoes are loaded with fiber and vitamin A. They are an excellent alternative to less nutritious sweet foods.

BAKED SWEET POTATOES

MAKES 6 SERVINGS (½ POTATO PER SERVING)

3 medium sweet potatoes (about 10 ounces each), washed
2 tablespoons reduced-fat margarine, or butter
1 teaspoon ground cinnamon

Preheat oven to 425°F.

Prick potatoes with the tip of a fork in a few places. Set on a nonstick cookie sheet. Bake potatoes for about 1 hour or until fork tender. Cool.

Cut potatoes in half lengthwise. Scoop out, leaving ½ inch of pulp around potato shell. Place pulp in a mixing bowl. Mix in margarine and cinnamon. Mash with a potato masher. Scoop mashed sweet potato back into the shells. Serve.

Per Serving: Calories: 73; % of calories from fat: 23; Fat (gm): 1.9; Saturated Fat (gm): 0.4; Cholesterol (mg): 0; Sodium (mg): 82; Protein (gm): 1.1; Carbohydrate (gm): 13.4 Exchanges: Milk: 0.0; Vegetable: 0.0; Fruit: 0.0; Bread: 1.0; Meat: 0.0; Fat: 0.0

Remind children to discard the shrimp tail. This dish is better suited to older children, who are less likely to hurt themselves (or their dining companions) with the skewers.

SHRIMP ON A STICK

MAKES 4 SERVINGS

4 short bamboo skewers
8 snow peas, trimmed
8 extra-large peeled and cooked shrimp
8 cherry tomatoes

Thread a snow pea, then a shrimp, and finally a tomato, onto each skewer. Repeat.

Place one skewer on each plate and serve.

....

Per Serving: Calories: 39; % of calories from fat: 13; Fat (gm): 0.6; Saturated Fat (gm): 0.1; Cholesterol (mg): 43.1; Sodium (mg): 43.9; Protein (gm): 6.2; Carbohydrate (gm): 2.1 Exchanges: Milk: 0.0; Vegetable: 0.0; Fruit: 0.0; Bread: 0.0; Meat: 1.0; Fat: 0.0

This dish is a labor-saving device for kids; the peas are "premushed" so they don't have to mash them up themselves.

Mushy Peas

MAKES 4 SERVINGS

2 cans (14½ ounces each) peas
2 tablespoons reduced-fat margarine
½ teaspoon ground tarragon
Salt and pepper, to taste

Heat peas in a saucepan for 5 minutes or until hot. Drain well and put in a bowl. Mash peas and margarine with a potato masher. Season with tarragon, salt, and pepper.

Serve hot.

Per Serving: Calories: 167; % of calories from fat: 18; Fat (gm): 3.5; Saturated Fat (gm): 0.7; Cholesterol (mg): 0; Sodium (mg): 587; Protein (gm): 9.2; Carbohydrate (gm): 26 Exchanges: Milk: 0.0; Vegetable: 0.0; Fruit: 0.0; Bread: 2.0; Meat: 0.0; Fat: 0.5

Bok choy, a member of the cabbage family, is rich in vitamins A and C and a good source of calcium and folic acid. Baby bok choy, available in some markets, is milder in flavor and likely to be more popular with kids.

STIR-FRIED VEGETABLES

MAKES 6 SERVINGS (1 ½ CUPS PER SERVING)

SAUCE:

¼ cup low-fat beef broth

1 tablespoon cornstarch

2 teaspoons reduced-sodium soy sauce

STIR-FRY:

Cooking spray

¾ cup chopped green onions

½ teaspoon chopped garlic

½ teaspoon chopped ginger

4 cups sliced bok choy

1 cup trimmed snow peas

1 cup sliced red and green bell peppers

In a small bowl, whisk together broth, cornstarch, and soy sauce. Set aside.

Heat a sprayed wok or large nonstick frying pan. Add onions and cook about 1 minute, stirring often. Season with garlic and ginger. Add bok choy and continue stirring over medium-high heat until just cooked, about 1 minute. Add snow peas and peppers. Cook another minute or two. Vegetables should be tender but still crisp. Stir in sauce and cook another minute, stirring often, until sauce thickens.

Serve hot. Good served over cooked whole-wheat rice or buckwheat noodles.

....

Per Serving: Calories: 29; % of calories from fat: 6; Fat (gm): 0.2; Saturated Fat (gm): 0.04; Cholesterol (mg): 0; Sodium (mg): 106; Protein (gm): 1.7; Carbohydrate (gm): 5.8 Exchanges: Milk: 0.0; Vegetable: 1.0; Fruit: 0.0; Bread: 0.0; Meat: 0.0; Fat: 0.0

Popcorn elevates the usual tomato soup to something far more interesting. Instead of popcorn you can float a few Goldfish crackers on top of the soup before serving.

TOMATO POPCORN SOUP

MAKES 6 SERVINGS

Butter-flavored cooking spray
½ cup chopped onions
1½ cups chopped tomatoes
2 cans (10¾ ounces each) condensed cream of tomato soup
Salt, pepper, and dried basil, to taste
3 cups plain popped corn

Heat a sprayed large saucepan over medium-low heat. Add onions and cook 4 to 5 minutes or until golden, stirring occasionally, and spraying the pan again if necessary.

Stir in tomatoes, tomato soup, and 3 cans of water. Bring soup to a boil, and reduce heat to simmer. Season with salt, pepper, and dried basil. Continue simmering for 10 to 15 minutes.

Ladle hot soup into bowls, garnish with popcorn and serve.

Per Serving: Calories: 102; % of calories from fat: 2; Fat (gm): 0.3; Saturated Fat (gm): 0.05; Cholesterol (mg): 0; Sodium (mg): 584; Protein (gm): 2.6; Carbohydrate (gm): 22.6 Exchanges: Milk: 0.0; Vegetable: 1.0; Fruit: 0.0; Bread: 1.0; Meat: 0.0; Fat: 0.0

10-MINUTE POPEYE SOUP

MAKES 6 TO 8 SERVINGS

Butter-flavored cooking spray
1 cup chopped onion
3 cups cooked, trimmed spinach
3 cups chicken broth
1 cup reduced-fat buttermilk, optional

In a sprayed nonstick saucepan, fry onions over medium heat for about 5 minutes, stirring occasionally. Add 1 to 2 tablespoons of broth if onions become too dry. Stir in spinach and chicken broth. Transfer soup to a food processor in batches. Puree until smooth. Return to saucepan.

Bring soup to a boil. Cook for 2 minutes, uncovered. When soup cools slightly, add buttermilk, if desired. You can add ½ cup of cooked pasta to the soup before serving.

....

Per Serving: Calories: 39; % of calories from fat: 10; Fat (gm): 0.5; Saturated Fat (gm): 0; Cholesterol (mg): 1.3; Sodium (mg): 544; Protein (gm): 3.4; Carbohydrate (gm): 6.6 Exchanges: Milk: 0.0; Vegetable: 1.0; Fruit: 0.0; Bread: 0.0; Meat: 0.0; Fat: 0.0

It is fun to serve soup in edible containers, such as the shells of pumpkins, squash, or melons. Save the cantaloupe shells and freeze them for reuse. Serve the soup in frozen shells.

SUMMER CANTALOUPE SOUP IN A SHELL

MAKES 6 SERVINGS

3 cups cubed cantaloupe
2 cups sugar-free ginger ale
¼ cup orange juice
¼ cup Splenda No Calorie Sweetener, or sugar

Puree ingredients in two batches. Using a food processor or blender, put in half of the cantaloupe. Add half of the ginger ale, orange juice, and sweetener. Puree, then pour into a bowl. Repeat with the remaining batch of ingredients, and add it to the same bowl. Refrigerate until ready to serve.

Pour mixture into soup bowls or frozen cantaloupe shells. Serve chilled. You may want to add 1 tablespoon of whipped nonfat dairy topping to each serving.

Per Serving: Calories: 32; % of calories from fat: 4; Fat (gm): 0.2; Saturated Fat (gm): 0; Cholesterol (mg): 0; Sodium (mg): 40; Protein (gm): 0.7; Carbohydrate (gm): 8.6 Exchanges: Milk: 0.0; Vegetable: 0.0; Fruit: 0.5; Bread: 0.0; Meat: 0.0; Fat: 0.0

The baby shrimp are a surprise inside each won ton.

WON TON SOUP

MAKES 4 SERVINGS (1 ¼ CUPS BROTH AND 1 WON TON PER
SERVING)

1 quart chicken broth

1 tablespoon cornstarch

½ cup finely chopped green onions

½ teaspoon ground ginger

4 won ton wrappers, available at large supermarkets and Asian
food stores

8 baby shrimp

Pour ½ cup chicken broth into a small bowl and stir in cornstarch. After
cornstarch has dissolved, pour mixture into a large saucepan and add
remaining chicken broth, green onions, and ground ginger. Heat broth over
medium heat until it comes to a boil. Reduce heat to simmer.

To make Won Tons: With the point of the wrapper facing you, add 2
shrimp. Fold up won ton. Moisten edges with water, and pinch together to
seal. Bring a small pan of water to a boil while the soup is simmering. Slide
won tons into water and cook for 1 minute. Remove with slotted spoon.
Slide won tons into simmering soup. Simmer 1 minute longer.

Serve 1 won ton in each bowl of soup.

Per Serving: Calories: 59; % of calories from fat: 14; Fat (gm): 0.9; Saturated Fat (gm): 0.1;
Cholesterol (mg): 24.3; Sodium (mg): 1001; Protein (gm): 4.6; Carbohydrate (gm): 7.6
Exchanges: Milk: 0.0; Vegetable: 0.0; Fruit: 0.0; Bread: 1.0; Meat: 0.0; Fat: 0.0

Just double your chili recipe next time you make it, and use half later for this delicious soup. If you like, sprinkle with grated reduced-fat cheese.

CHILI SOUP

MAKES 4 SERVINGS (½ CUP SOUP PLUS ¼ CUP CHILI)

2 cans (14 ounces each) beef broth

1 cup chopped tomatoes

1 cup Cowboy Bill's Turkey Chili (see recipe on page 105)

½ teaspoon chili powder

Pour beef broth into a saucepan. Mix in chopped tomatoes, chili, and chili powder.

Bring soup to a boil, reduce heat to simmer. Continue cooking, uncovered, for 2 minutes or until soup is heated.

Serve in individual soup bowls.

....

Per Serving: Calories: 83; % of calories from fat: 29; Fat (gm): 2.6; Saturated Fat (gm): 0.6; Cholesterol (mg): 14.5; Sodium (mg): 856; Protein (gm): 7.4; Carbohydrate (gm): 7.4 Exchanges: Milk: 0.0; Vegetable: 0.0; Fruit: 0.0; Bread: 0.5; Meat: 1.0; Fat: 0.0

CHAPTER SIX

MAIN DISHES

Pasta takes on a whole new dimension when it's fried.

FRIED TORTELLINI

MAKES 6 SERVINGS (2 TORTELLINI PER SERVING)

12 squash, spinach, or other vegetable-filled freezer tortellini
2 tablespoons olive oil
Olive oil-flavored cooking spray
¼ cup chopped parsley
¼ cup grated carrots
¼ cup chopped green onions, optional

Cook tortellini according to package directions. Usually, add tortellini to boiling water and cook 8 to 10 minutes. Drain well.

Heat oil in a sprayed nonstick frying pan. Add cooked tortellini and fry over medium heat for 1 to 2 minutes on each side, until golden brown.

Remove to serving dish, and sprinkle with parsley, carrots, and onions.

Per Serving: Calories: 104; % of calories from fat: 50; Fat (gm): 6.1; Saturated Fat (gm): 1.4; Cholesterol (mg): 8; Sodium (mg): 91; Protein (gm): 3.3; Carbohydrate (gm): 10.3 Exchanges: Milk: 0.0; Vegetable: 0.0; Fruit: 0.0; Bread: 1.0; Meat: 0.0; Fat: 1.0

I call these dinosaur meatballs because they're larger than standard meatballs.

DINOSAUR MEATBALLS

MAKES 4 SERVINGS (1 MEATBALL PER SERVING)

1 pound lean ground turkey, or pork
1 teaspoon ground Italian spice mix
¼ cup Italian-flavored bread crumbs
¼ cup egg substitute, or 1 egg

Preheat oven to 450°F.

Using a mixing bowl, combine ground turkey, seasoning, bread crumbs, and egg substitute. Shape mixture into 4 large balls, using hands or ice cream scooper. Arrange meatballs on an ungreased cookie sheet.

Bake in center of oven for 30 minutes or until cooked through. Turn oven up to broil, and broil meatballs for 2 minutes, until browned. Or pan fry meatballs in nonstick frying pan coated with cooking spray.

Serve hot. These are cute served centered on a bed of whole-wheat spaghetti and drizzled with 2 tablespoons of spaghetti sauce.

....

Per Serving: Calories: 153; % of calories from fat: 11; Fat (gm): 1.9; Saturated Fat (gm): 0.5; Cholesterol (mg): 45; Sodium (mg): 289; Protein (gm): 28.3; Carbohydrate (gm): 5 Exchanges: Milk: 0.0; Vegetable: 0.0; Fruit: 0.0; Bread: 0.0; Meat: 3.0; Fat: 0.0

EASY ARROZ CON POLLO (CHICKEN WITH RICE)

MAKES 8 SERVINGS

1 pound skinless, boneless chicken breast, cut into halves
½ teaspoon ground cumin
½ teaspoon dried oregano
Olive oil-flavored cooking spray
1 cup sliced onion
3 cups cooked brown rice
1 cup canned green peas, drained
Salt and pepper, to taste

Wash chicken and blot dry. Combine cumin and oregano. Spray chicken with cooking spray and rub with spices.

Heat a large nonstick frying pan coated with cooking spray over medium heat. Add onion and chicken breasts. Cook 3 to 5 minutes on each side or until chicken is cooked through. Remove chicken from pan and cut into ½-inch pieces.

In sprayed frying pan, mix rice and chicken pieces together with onions and peas. Season to taste with salt and pepper. Cook until heated through, stirring once or twice.

Serve hot on individual plates.

....

Per Serving: Calories: 167; % of calories from fat: 8; Fat (gm): 1.5; Saturated Fat (gm): 0.3; Cholesterol (mg): 32.9; Sodium (mg): 88; Protein (gm): 16.1; Carbohydrate (gm): 21.6
Exchanges: Milk: 0.0; Vegetable: 0.0; Fruit: 0.0; Bread: 1.0; Meat: 2.0; Fat: 0.0

This chicken tastes great served with a small dollop of light sour cream.

CAMPFIRE CHICKEN AND ROASTED POTATOES

MAKES 6 SERVINGS

Butter-flavored cooking spray
6 small chicken drumsticks, skin removed
3 tablespoons Chili Spice (recipe follows)
1 recipe Roasted Potatoes (see recipe on page 96)

Preheat oven to 400°F. Spray a cookie sheet with butter-flavored cooking spray.

Spray chicken. Sprinkle drumsticks with chili spice, patting it to adhere to drumstick.

Arrange drumsticks on cookie sheet. Bake in center of oven for 45 minutes or until chicken is no longer pink and juices run clear when cut with a small knife. Let chicken cool 5 minutes before serving with Roasted Potatoes (see recipe on page 96).

CHILI SPICE

MAKES ¼ CUP SPICE

2 tablespoons mild chili powder
1 tablespoon ground cumin
2 teaspoons onion flakes
1 teaspoon garlic powder
½ teaspoon black pepper

Combine chili powder, cumin, onion flakes, garlic powder, and pepper in a small bowl. Place in a covered container and store at room temperature.

COMPLETE RECIPE Per Serving: Calories: 225; % of calories from fat: 27; Fat (gm): 6.7; Saturated Fat (gm): 1.4; Cholesterol (mg): 78.5; Sodium (mg): 115; Protein (gm): 23; Carbohydrate (gm): 17.7 Exchanges: Milk: 0.0; Vegetable: 0.0; Fruit: 0.0; Bread: 1.0; Meat: 3.0; Fat: 0.0

Potatoes are a good source of vitamin C, potassium, fiber, iron, and niacin.

ROASTED POTATOES

MAKES 6 SERVINGS

Olive oil-flavored cooking spray
3 cups cubed potatoes, skin on
2 tablespoons sugar-free vinegar and oil salad dressing

Preheat oven to 450°F. Spray a roasting pan.

Toss potatoes with salad dressing in a bowl. Arrange potatoes in roasting pan. Bake potatoes for 45 minutes or until tender. Serve hot.

....

ROASTED POTATOES ONLY Per Serving: Calories: 90; % of calories from fat: 26; Fat (gm): 2.7; Saturated Fat (gm): 0.5; Cholesterol (mg): 0; Sodium (mg): 4; Protein (gm): 1.3; Carbohydrate (gm): 15.7 Exchanges: Milk: 0.0; Vegetable: 0.0; Fruit: 0.0; Bread: 1.0; Meat: 0.0; Fat: 0.5

A frittata is an open-face omelet that is good hot, cold, or at room temperature. Try it with various toppings—whatever veggies your children like.

VEGGIE FRITTATA

MAKES 6 SERVINGS

2 cups egg substitute, or 8 eggs
¼ cup reduced-fat (2%) milk
Salt and pepper, to taste
¾ cup shredded reduced-fat Swiss cheese
1 cup cooked trimmed asparagus, cut into 1-inch pieces
1 cup frozen, drained peas
Olive oil-flavored cooking spray
2 tablespoons reduced-fat margarine, or butter

In a large bowl, whisk egg substitute, milk, salt, and pepper until blended. Stir in cheese, asparagus, and peas.

Preheat broiler.

Melt margarine in a large, sprayed nonstick frying pan with ovenproof handle.

Over medium heat, carefully pour in egg mixture. Lift edges as egg firms and allow uncooked egg to flow under until the bottom is a golden brown and the center is still a little runny, about 3 to 4 minutes. Shake frying pan occasionally, making sure frittata isn't sticking to bottom.

Place pan under the broiler for 1 to 2 minutes, until top of frittata is light golden brown. Invert onto a serving dish or serve from the pan. Cut into wedges.

....

Per Serving: Calories: 114; % of calories from fat: 23; Fat (gm): 2.9; Saturated Fat (gm): 1; Cholesterol (mg): 5.5; Sodium (mg): 261; Protein (gm): 14.4; Carbohydrate (gm): 7.4 Exchanges: Milk: 0.0; Vegetable: 0.0; Fruit: 0.0; Bread: 0.0; Meat: 2.0; Fat: 0.0

Serve these eggs with small whole-wheat bagel halves. I love Nova lox, but you can use another type of cured, or even smoked, salmon if you prefer.

EGGS WITH LOX AND ONION

MAKES 4 SERVINGS

Butter-flavored cooking spray
2 tablespoons reduced-fat margarine
1 cup sliced onions
½ cup chopped Nova lox
2 cups egg substitute plus 2 egg whites, or 8 eggs plus 2 egg whites
¼ cup nonfat milk
Salt and white pepper, to taste

Heat a sprayed nonstick frying pan and melt the margarine over medium heat. Add onions and cook for about 5 minutes, stirring occasionally, until onions have begun to brown. Stir in lox.

In a bowl, whisk egg substitute and egg whites with milk, salt, and pepper. Pour egg mixture over onions and lox. Cook, stirring and folding the eggs together with onions and lox, until just cooked through.

Divide onto individual plates and serve hot.

....

Per Serving: Calories: 132; % of calories from fat: 26; Fat (gm): 3.8; Saturated Fat (gm): 0.8; Cholesterol (mg): 5.2; Sodium (mg): 732; Protein (gm): 16.8; Carbohydrate (gm): 6.8 Exchanges: Milk: 0.0; Vegetable: 1.0; Fruit: 0.0; Bread: 0.0; Meat: 2.0; Fat: 0.0

Greek chicken is made lovingly with the best olive oil and freshly squeezed lemon juice.

GREEK CHICKEN

MAKES 6 SERVINGS

2 fresh lemons
Olive oil-flavored cooking spray
6 boned chicken legs, skin discarded
2 tablespoons extra-virgin olive oil
1 tablespoon dried oregano

Cut 1 lemon in half. Thinly slice the other lemon. Set aside.

Preheat oven to 425°F. Lightly coat a shallow baking pan with cooking spray.

Place chicken in pan and brush with olive oil and juice from halved lemon. Sprinkle with oregano and lemon slices.

Bake chicken in center of oven for 50 to 60 minutes or until chicken is no longer pink in the center when cut with a small knife. Remove from the oven and serve hot.

....

Per Serving: Calories: 201; % of calories from fat: 44; Fat (gm): 9.5; Saturated Fat (gm): 1.9; Cholesterol (mg): 104; Sodium (mg): 112; Protein (gm): 26.3; Carbohydrate (gm): 1.4 Exchanges: Milk: 0.0; Vegetable: 0.0; Fruit: 0.0; Bread: 0.0; Meat: 3.5; Fat: 0.0

No need to stuff your child with fast-food burgers when you can make healthier versions at home.

GRILLED BURGER WITH ALL THE TRIMMINGS

MAKES 4 SERVINGS (1 HAMBURGER PER SERVING)

1 pound (90% lean) ground beef

½ cup chopped onions

2 egg whites

Salt, pepper, and garlic powder, to taste

2 small hamburger rolls, split in half

4 leaves romaine lettuce, washed and drained

4 slices tomato

8 pickle slices

In a bowl, combine ground beef, onions, and egg whites. Season with salt, pepper, and garlic powder. Divide mixture evenly, and shape into 4 burgers. Place on a plate, cover, and refrigerate until ready to grill.

Preheat stovetop or electric indoor grill according to manufacturer's instructions, use broiler, or fire up outdoor grill if weather permits. Grill meat about 6 to 8 minutes, turning once, until cooked through.

Place a lettuce leaf on each half roll. Place burger on lettuce and top with tomato and pickle slices. Serve with mustard and catsup.

....

Per Serving: Calories: 237; % of calories from fat: 24; Fat (gm): 6.2; Saturated Fat (gm): 2; Cholesterol (mg): 65; Sodium (mg): 344; Protein (gm): 29.3; Carbohydrate (gm): 14.3 Exchanges: Milk: 0.0; Vegetable: 0.0; Fruit: 0.0; Bread: 1.0; Meat: 3.0; Fat: 0.0

Piled-High Baked Potatoes

MAKES 4 SERVINGS (1 POTATO PER SERVING; FOR YOUNG
CHILDREN, CUT POTATO IN HALF)

4 baking potatoes, about ½ pound each

4 teaspoons reduced-fat margarine

2 cups shredded lettuce

1 cup chopped tomatoes

1 cup Gooey Sloppy Joes (see recipe on page 65)

½ cup chopped onions, optional

1 cup fat-free sour cream

Wash potatoes and prick with a fork or tip of a small knife. Bake potatoes in a 425°F oven for 1 hour or until fork tender; or cook in a microwave on High for about 10 to 15 minutes, depending on the size of the potatoes and the microwave.

Open potatoes and fluff up pulp with a fork. Spread 1 teaspoon margarine on each potato. Sprinkle each potato with lettuce, tomatoes, and hot Sloppy Joe mixture. Sprinkle potatoes with onions (if using) and a dollop of sour cream.

Per Serving: Calories: 390; % of calories from fat: 8; Fat (gm): 3.5; Saturated Fat (gm): 0.8; Cholesterol (mg): 40; Sodium (mg): 490; Protein (gm): 28; Carbohydrate (gm): 63.3 Exchanges: Milk: 0.0; Vegetable: 0.0; Fruit: 0.0; Bread: 4.0; Meat: 2.0; Fat: 0.0

These prepared chickens are excellent for times when you're rushed. Remember to discard the skin. Rotisserie chickens are also good for chicken salad or eating on the bone. You can customize them in seconds with a sauce of your choice.

CUSTOMIZED ROTISSERIE CHICKEN

MAKES 8 SERVINGS

1 purchased rotisserie chicken (about 5 pounds), skin discarded
⅓ cup plain fat-free yogurt
1½ teaspoons barbecue sauce

With poultry shears or knife, cut chicken into 8 serving pieces. Preheat oven to 350°F. Mix together yogurt and barbecue sauce. Brush chicken with mixture and place on a cookie sheet.

Warm chicken in oven for 5 minutes. Serve with salad or coleslaw.

Per Serving: Calories: 286; % of calories from fat: 37; Fat (gm): 11.1; Saturated Fat (gm): 3; Cholesterol (mg): 125.7; Sodium (mg): 141; Protein (gm): 42; Carbohydrate (gm): 0.9 Exchanges: Milk: 0.0; Vegetable: 0.0; Fruit: 0.0; Bread: 0.0; Meat: 5.0; Fat: 0.0

Wild turkeys were native to the United States, Mexico, and Central America. The early settlers sent some of these then-domesticated birds back to Europe. Before long, the Europeans were breeding them into a plumper version. Once again they were transported across the ocean, this time back to the New World, and crossbred into the modern variety.

TURKEY PICK-UP STICKS

MAKES 6 SERVINGS

1½ pounds ground skinless turkey breast

2 tablespoons dried onion flakes

1 teaspoon Worcestershire sauce

1 egg white

12 wooden skewers, soaked in water 20 minutes, drained

Butter-flavored cooking spray

Combine ground turkey, onion flakes, Worcestershire sauce, and egg white in a bowl. Wipe skewers. Using clean hands, mold about ¼ cup turkey mixture around each skewer. Cover tips of skewers with foil to keep them from charring.

Preheat stovetop or electric indoor grill according to manufacturer's instructions, use broiler, or fire up outdoor grill if weather permits. Grill or broil turkey about 8 to 10 minutes, turning as needed, until cooked through. Serve hot with mustard and chopped tomatoes.

....

Per Serving: Calories: 130; % of calories from fat: 11; Fat (gm): 1.5; Saturated Fat (gm): 0.5; Cholesterol (mg): 45; Sodium (mg): 93; Protein (gm): 27; Carbohydrate (gm): 1.6 Exchanges: Milk: 0.0; Vegetable: 0.0; Fruit: 0.0; Bread: 0.0; Meat: 3.0; Fat: 0.0

Salmon is an excellent source of healthful omega-3 fatty acid.

FISH STRIPS

MAKES 6 SERVINGS

> Butter-flavored cooking spray
> 2 egg whites, lightly beaten
> ½ cup seasoned bread crumbs
> 1 pound skinless salmon fillet, cut crosswise into 12 slices

Preheat oven to 425°F. Spray a cookie sheet.

Arrange egg whites in a shallow bowl and bread crumbs in another. Roll salmon strips in egg whites, then in bread crumbs. Set fish strips on prepared cookie sheet.

Bake salmon strips in center of oven for 10 minutes or until fish flakes easily when prodded with a fork.

....

Per Serving: Calories: 182; % of calories from fat: 44; Fat (gm): 8.7; Saturated Fat (gm): 1.8; Cholesterol (mg): 44.3; Sodium (mg): 239; Protein (gm): 17.7; Carbohydrate (gm): 6.9 Exchanges: Milk: 0.0; Vegetable: 0.0; Fruit: 0.0; Bread: 0.5; Meat: 2.0; Fat: 1.0

COWBOY BILL'S TURKEY CHILI

MAKES 9 SERVINGS (1 CUP PER SERVING)

Olive oil-flavored cooking spray

2 cups chopped onions

1½ cups ground turkey

1 can (15 ounces) pinto beans, including liquid

1 can (15 ounces) kidney beans, drained

1 can (15 ounces) chopped tomatoes, including liquid

2 tablespoons chili powder

1 teaspoon ground cumin

½ teaspoon garlic powder

Grated reduced-fat cheese, optional

Spray a heavy saucepan. Add onions and cook over medium heat for 5 minutes, stirring occasionally. Mix in turkey, beans, and tomatoes. Add chili powder, cumin, and garlic powder.

Cook for 20 minutes over medium-low heat, stirring occasionally. Taste toward end of cooking time and adjust seasonings if desired. Serve hot.

Sprinkle with a small amount of cheese, if using.

....

Per Serving: Calories: 248; % of calories from fat: 31; Fat (gm): 8.4; Saturated Fat (gm): 2.1; Cholesterol (mg): 57.8; Sodium (mg): 457; Protein (gm): 21.1; Carbohydrate (gm): 21.6 Exchanges: Milk: 0.0; Vegetable: 0.0; Fruit: 0.0; Bread: 1.5; Meat: 2.5; Fat: 0.0

Chicken Sausages with Apples

MAKES 6 SERVINGS

4 lean chicken sausages (preferably made with apple)
Butter-flavored cooking spray
2 tablespoons reduced-fat margarine
4 firm apples such as Golden Delicious, peeled, cored, and sliced

In a saucepan, cover sausages with water. Bring water to a boil, reduce heat to low, and simmer sausages for 10 minutes or according to package direction. Slice in coin shapes and set aside.

Heat margarine in a sprayed nonstick frying pan. Pan fry apples for about 4 minutes, turning as necessary until a light golden brown. Add sausages and cook until lightly browned, stirring as needed.

Serve on individual plates and garnish with cucumber wedges, if desired.

....

Per Serving: Calories: 138; % of calories from fat: 27; Fat (gm): 4.4; Saturated Fat (gm): 1.1; Cholesterol (mg): 46.7; Sodium (mg): 460; Protein (gm): 11.6; Carbohydrate (gm): 14.7
Exchanges: Milk: 0.0; Vegetable: 0.0; Fruit: 1.0; Bread: 0.0; Meat: 1.5; Fat: 0.0

HOMEMADE TURKEY SAUSAGES

MAKES 8 SERVINGS

1¼ pounds ground turkey
1 egg white
⅓ cup minced green onion
¼ cup ground parsley
½ teaspoon dried marjoram
½ teaspoon dried sage
Salt and pepper, to taste
Olive oil-flavored cooking spray

Crumble turkey into a bowl. Mix in egg white, green onions, parsley, marjoram, and sage. Add salt and pepper to taste.

Shape turkey mixture into 2-inch-long sausages.

Heat a sprayed nonstick frying pan over medium heat. Pan fry sausages until cooked, turning with a spatula as needed. Sausages will brown slightly and should be cooked through. Remove to a serving dish.

Serve with eggs or pancakes for that very special breakfast, lunch, or dinner.

....

Per Serving: Calories: 111; % of calories from fat: 50; Fat (gm): 6; Saturated Fat (gm): 1.6; Cholesterol (mg): 56; Sodium (mg): 59; Protein (gm): 13; Carbohydrate (gm): 0.5 Exchanges: Milk: 0.0; Vegetable: 0.0; Fruit: 0.0; Bread: 0.0; Meat: 2.0; Fat: 0.0

If you are serving this dish to teenagers, you might want to add ½ teaspoon of curry powder to the sauce.

ALOHA CHICKEN

MAKES 4 SERVINGS

1 cup mango fat-free yogurt
¼ cup minced fresh cilantro
½ cup canned pineapple tidbits, packed in fruit juice, drained
Butter-flavored cooking spray
1 pound (4 pieces) boneless, skinless chicken breasts

In a small bowl, mix mango yogurt with cilantro and pineapple tidbits. Cover and refrigerate until needed. Stir sauce before serving.

Heat a sprayed frying pan over medium heat. Fry the chicken breasts (or use a stove-top grill or electric grill) until just cooked through, turning as necessary, about 8 to 10 minutes, depending on thickness of chicken. Chicken will be slightly firm to the touch, and juices will run clear when pierced with knife.

Serve chicken hot, drizzled with mango yogurt sauce.

....

Per Serving: Calories: 154; % of calories from fat: 8; Fat (gm): 1.4; Saturated Fat (gm): 0.4; Cholesterol (mg): 65.7; Sodium (mg): 68; Protein (gm): 26.8; Carbohydrate (gm): 7.1 Exchanges: Milk: 0.0; Vegetable: 0.0; Fruit: 0.5; Bread: 0.0; Meat: 3.0; Fat: 0.0

You can substitute sweet potatoes for the white potatoes. If you like you can sprinkle the potatoes with ½ teaspoon of dried rosemary. Potato wedges will be crusty and soft on the inside. Fun served with hamburgers.

HOME FRIES

MAKES 4 SERVINGS

Olive oil-flavored nonstick cooking spray
2 baking potatoes, skins intact, thoroughly washed
2 tablespoons canola oil
½ teaspoon garlic powder

Place rack in center of oven and preheat to 425°F. Spray a baking sheet with cooking spray.

Slice potatoes in wedges and arrange on baking sheet. Brush potatoes with oil and sprinkle with garlic powder.

Bake potatoes for 45 minutes, turning once, until tender.

....

Per Serving: Calories: 155; % of calories from fat: 40; Fat (gm): 7.1; Saturated Fat (gm): 0.5; Cholesterol (mg): 0; Sodium (mg): 10; Protein (gm): 2.6; Carbohydrate (gm): 21.6 Exchanges: Milk: 0.0; Vegetable: 0.0; Fruit: 0.0; Bread: 1.5; Meat: 0.0; Fat: 1.0.

Have the children help make this dish. It is fast and fun to create.

CALIFORNIA ROLLS WITH TURKEY

MAKES 5 SERVINGS OF 4 SLICES (20 SLICES)

1 cup reduced-fat ricotta cheese

2 11-inch flour tortillas

2 cups baby spinach of lettuce leaves, washed

1 cup chopped green onion

1 cup alfalfa sprouts

4 ounces thinly sliced turkey breast

Spread ½ cup of cheese evenly over each tortilla to within ¼-inch of edge.

Starting 1 inch from bottom edges, layer ½ of the spinach, onion, alfalfa sprouts, and turkey evenly over ⅔ of each tortilla.

Starting from the bottom. roll up tortillas jelly-roll style. Wrap in plastic wrap; refrigerate for 1 hour. When ready to serve, unwrap and cut each roll crosswise into 10 1-inch slices.

....

Per Serving: Calories: 219; % of calories from fat: 24; Fat (gm): 5.9; Saturated Fat (gm): 2.5; Cholesterol (mg): 34.8; Sodium (mg): 471; Protein (gm): 16.9; Carbohydrate (gm): 24.8 Exchanges: Milk: 0.0; Vegetable: 0.0; Fruit: 0.5; Bread: 1.5; Meat: 2.0; Fat: 0.0.

CHAPTER SEVEN

MUFFINS AND CUPCAKES

Little touches, such as turning muffins into "bunnies," count for a lot with children.

BLUEBERRY MUFFINS WITH BUNNY EARS

MAKES 12 MUFFINS (1 PER SERVING)

¼ cup reduced-fat margarine, or butter, at room temperature
⅓ cup Splenda No Calorie Sweetener, or sugar
½ cup egg substitute, or 2 eggs
1½ cups sifted all-purpose flour
½ cup sifted whole-wheat flour
4 teaspoons baking powder
⅔ cup nonfat milk
1 cup fresh blueberries, washed and drained on paper towels
24 almond slices

Preheat oven to 400°F. Line a muffin pan with paper liners.

With an electric mixer, cream margarine and sweetener together. Mix in egg substitute.

In a separate bowl, mix together flours and baking powder. Add flour mixture alternately with milk to margarine mixture. Gently stir in berries.

Spoon batter into muffin pan, filling cups ⅔ full. Bake in center of oven for 20 minutes or until cake tester or wooden pick inserted into center of muffin comes out clean. Cool in pan 5 minutes, then remove to wire rack.

Stick two almonds upright in each muffin to resemble bunny ears. Serve warm or cold.

....

Per Serving: Calories: 123; % of calories from fat: 25; Fat (gm): 3.5; Saturated Fat (gm): 0.5; Cholesterol (mg): 0.3; Sodium (mg): 234; Protein (gm): 4.4; Carbohydrate (gm): 19.8 Exchanges: Milk: 0.0; Vegetable: 0.0; Fruit: 0.0; Bread: 1.0; Meat: 0.0; Fat: 1.0

Cocoa adds character to traditional bran muffins. Cool, cover, and freeze muffins for later use.

COCOA MUFFINS

MAKES 10 MUFFINS (1 PER SERVING)

1½ cups bran cereal

1¼ cups nonfat milk

2 egg whites, lightly beaten

2 tablespoons reduced-fat margarine, melted

1¼ cups all-purpose flour

3 tablespoons unsweetened cocoa powder

⅓ cup Splenda No Calorie Sweetener

1 tablespoon baking soda

Preheat oven to 400°F. Line a muffin pan with paper liners.

In a mixing bowl, blend cereal with milk. Stir in egg whites and margarine. Blend in flour, cocoa, sweetener, and baking soda.

Spoon heaping ½ cup of batter into each prepared muffin cup. Bake in center of oven for 15 to 20 minutes or until muffins are golden brown and cake tester or toothpick inserted into center of muffin comes out clean.

Cool muffins 5 minutes in pan, then remove to wire rack. Serve warm or cold.

....

Per Serving: Calories: 108; % of calories from fat: 13; Fat (gm): 1.8; Saturated Fat (gm): 0.4; Cholesterol (mg): 0.6; Sodium (mg): 454; Protein (gm): 4.9; Carbohydrate (gm): 22.1 Exchanges: Milk: 0.0; Vegetable: 0.0; Fruit: 0.0; Bread: 1.5; Meat: 0.0; Fat: 0.0

We all know that the top of the muffin is the best part. How many of us just eat the muffin tops? Home goods stores sell pans to make just muffin tops. If you don't have one of these, you'll either need two pans, or you can bake in two batches.

Chocolate Chip Muffin Tops

MAKES 24 MUFFIN TOPS (1 PER SERVING)

Butter-flavored cooking spray

¼ cup reduced-fat margarine, or butter, at room temperature

⅓ cup Splenda No Calorie Sweetener, or sugar

½ cup egg substitute, or 2 eggs, lightly beaten

2 cups cake flour, sifted

4 teaspoons baking powder

⅔ cup nonfat milk

48 semisweet chocolate chips, or white chocolate chips

Preheat oven to 400°F. Lightly spray a muffin-top pan with butter-flavored spray.

Using an electric mixer, cream margarine and sweetener. Mix in egg substitute.

Mix together flour and baking powder in a separate bowl. Add flour mixture alternately with milk to the margarine mixture. Gently stir in chocolate chips.

Spoon batter into muffin-top pan, filling each cup to the top. Bake in center of oven for 15 to 20 minutes or until cake tester or toothpick inserted into muffin top comes out clean. Cool 5 minutes, then remove from pan.

....

Per Serving: Calories: 55; % of calories from fat: 25; Fat (gm): 1.6; Saturated Fat (gm): 0.5; Cholesterol (mg): 0.1; Sodium (mg): 117; Protein (gm): 1.6; Carbohydrate (gm): 9.2 Exchanges: Milk: 0.0; Vegetable: 0.0; Fruit: 0.0; Bread: 0.5; Meat: 0.0; Fat: 0.5

It's fun to watch a child open a popover and ask, "What happened to the inside? Where did it go?" It's like magic.

POPOVERS

MAKES 8 POPOVERS (1 PER SERVING)

½ cup egg substitute, or 2 eggs, lightly beaten

1 cup whole milk

1 cup all-purpose flour, sifted

1 tablespoon reduced-fat margarine, or butter, melted

Butter-flavored cooking spray

Preheat oven to 475°F. Using an electric mixer, beat egg substitute, milk, and flour until foamy, about 2 minutes. Beat in cooled melted margarine for about 20 seconds.

Preheat muffin pan in oven for 5 minutes. Remove hot pan, using potholders. Spray cup forms in pan. Pour batter into 8 of the muffin cups. Bake on top rack of oven for 15 minutes.

Reduce temperature to 350°F., and continue baking for 30 minutes longer or until popovers are golden and puffy. They are done when cutting a small slit in one with a knife releases steam.

....

Per Serving: Calories: 89; % of calories from fat: 19; Fat (gm): 1.8; Saturated Fat (gm): 0.7; Cholesterol (mg): 3.1; Sodium (mg): 59; Protein (gm): 4.1; Carbohydrate (gm): 13.6 Exchanges: Milk: 0.0; Vegetable: 0.0; Fruit: 0.0; Bread: 1.0; Meat: 0.0; Fat: 0.05

These cute "angels" illustrate just how easy it is to turn a standard dessert into something special.

ANGEL CUPCAKES

MAKES 20 CUPCAKES (1 PER SERVING)

> 1 package (1.4 ounces) instant sugar-free vanilla pudding mix
> 2 cups nonfat milk
> 1 package (18.25 ounces) white cake mix
> 1⅓ cups water
> 3 egg whites
> 2 tablespoons canola oil

Pour pudding mix into a small bowl. Whisk in milk and stir until smooth. Set aside for pudding to set.

Preheat oven to 350°F. Line muffin pans with cupcake liners, or spray with butter-flavored cooking spray.

Using an electric mixer, beat cake mix with water, egg whites, and oil. Mix for 2 to 3 minutes or until smooth.

Pour batter evenly into prepared cupcake liners, filling cups a scant ⅔ full. Bake in center of oven for 20 to 25 minutes or until a toothpick inserted into center of cupcake comes out dry.

Let cupcakes stand 5 minutes, then remove to wire rack to cool. When cool, carefully cut off about a ½-inch-thick slice from the top of each cupcake with a small, sharp knife and reserve. Using a spoon, scoop out about 1 tablespoon of cupcake from the center of each and discard. Spoon vanilla pudding into each cavity and spread some over remaining cupcake. Cut "lid" of each cupcake in half, and arrange pieces upright and back-to-back in the center of each cupcake to resemble wings.

....

Per Serving: Calories: 140; % of calories from fat: 27; Fat (gm): 4.2; Saturated Fat (gm): 0.6; Cholesterol (mg): 0.5; Sodium (mg): 228; Protein (gm): 2.5; Carbohydrate (gm): 23 Exchanges: Milk: 0.0; Vegetable: 0.0; Fruit: 0.0; Bread: 1.5; Meat: 0.0; Fat: 1.0

You can use different pie fillings in these mini-cupcakes if you like. Try blueberry or peach in addition to or instead of cherry.

CHERRY CUPCAKES

MAKES 48 MINI-CUPCAKES (2 PER SERVING)

1 package (18.25 ounces) white cake mix
1 cup water
2 tablespoons canola oil
3 egg whites
¾ cup canned light cherry pie filling

Preheat oven to 350°F. Line 2 mini-muffin pans with mini-paper liners.

With an electric mixer, beat cake mix with water (or as package recommends), oil, and egg whites for 3 minutes (or according to package directions) to make a smooth batter.

Pour batter into muffin pans, filling each paper cup about ½ full. Bake in center of oven for about 15 minutes or until a toothpick inserted into center of cupcake comes out clean.

Remove cupcakes from oven and cool. Using a teaspoon, scoop out a cavity about ½ inch deep in center of each cupcake and discard. Fill cavity with 1 teaspoonful of cherry pie filling. Pat down filling with back of spoon.

....

Per Serving: Calories: 110; % of calories from fat: 29; Fat (gm): 3.5; Saturated Fat (gm): 0.4; Cholesterol (mg): 0; Sodium (mg): 151; Protein (gm): 1.4; Carbohydrate (gm): 18.2 Exchanges: Milk: 0.0; Vegetable: 0.0; Fruit: 0.0; Bread: 1.0; Meat: 0.0; Fat: 1.0

Cupcakes freeze well. What a great treat to store away for a rainy day.

MINI CHOCOLATE CUPCAKES

MAKES 20 CUPCAKES (1 PER SERVING)

1 cup all-purpose flour

⅓ cup Splenda No Calorie Sweetener

¼ cup unsweetened cocoa

1½ teaspoons baking powder

¼ cup egg substitute

½ cup plus 2 tablespoons reduced-fat (2%) milk

⅓ cup canola oil

1¼ teaspoons vanilla extract

Preheat oven to 350°F. Line 2 mini-muffin pans with mini-paper liners.

In a mixing bowl, whisk together flour, sweetener, cocoa, and baking powder. In another bowl, combine egg substitute, milk, oil, and vanilla. Stir dry ingredients into milk mixture.

Fill each paper liner ⅔ full. Bake in center of oven for about 15 to 18 minutes or until a toothpick inserted into a cupcake comes out clean. Cool 5 minutes, then remove from pans and cool completely on a rack.

Sprinkle lightly with confectioner's sugar if desired.

....

Per Serving: Calories: 63; % of calories from fat: 53; Fat (gm): 4; Saturated Fat (gm): 0.4; Cholesterol (mg): 0.6; Sodium (mg): 45.8; Protein (gm): 1.4; Carbohydrate (gm): 6.3 Exchanges: Milk: 0.0; Vegetable: 0.0; Fruit: 0.0; Bread: 0.5; Meat: 0.0; Fat: 0.5

These are lots of fun for a birthday. Have the children help make them.

ICE CREAM CONE CUPCAKES

MAKES 8 SERVINGS

8 plain flat-bottom ice cream cones
½ of an 18.25-ounce package yellow, or lemon, cake mix
3 tablespoons reduced-fat cottage cheese
2 tablespoons canola oil
¾ cup egg substitute
2 teaspoons colored sprinkles

Preheat oven to 350°F. Place cones in cups of a muffin pan.

Using an electric mixer, beat cake mix with cottage cheese, oil, and egg substitute, beating according to package instructions. Pour enough batter into each cone to fill it ½ full. Bake in center of oven for about 10 to 15 minutes or until cake tester or toothpick inserted into cupcake comes out clean. Remove from oven and sprinkle each cone cupcake with sprinkles. Let cool.

....

Per Serving: Calories: 231; % of calories from fat: 31; Fat (gm): 7.9; Saturated Fat (gm): 0.9; Cholesterol (mg): 1.1; Sodium (mg): 309; Protein (gm): 5.2; Carbohydrate (gm): 35 Exchanges: Milk: 0.0; Vegetable: 0.0; Fruit: 0.0; Bread: 2.0; Meat: 0.0; Fat: 1.5

CHAPTER EIGHT

SWEET TREATS AND DESSERTS

Apple Betty is an old New England recipe. It is simply a graham cracker crust with an applesauce filling.

APPLE BETTY PIE

MAKES 8 SERVINGS

3 cups purchased no-sugar-added applesauce, or 1 recipe
   Raspberry Apple Sauce (see recipe on page 123)
1 (9-inch) Graham Cracker Crust (see recipe on page 124)
¼ cup graham cracker crumbs
½ cup sugar-free, nondairy whipped topping

Preheat oven to 350°F.

Spoon applesauce into prepared crust. Sprinkle with graham cracker crumbs. Bake in center of oven for 15 minutes. Remove pie and cool for about 15 minutes. Pie is best served warm.

Serve on individual plates, and top each serving with 1 tablespoon whipping topping.

Per Serving: Calories: 139; % of calories from fat: 31; Fat (gm): 4.8; Saturated Fat (gm): 1.1; Cholesterol (mg): 0; Sodium (mg): 210; Protein (gm): 2; Carbohydrate (gm): 22.4 Exchanges: Milk: 0.0; Vegetable: 0.0; Fruit: 0.5; Bread: 1.0; Meat: 0.0; Fat: 1.0

This is a chunky applesauce. If you prefer a finer sauce or don't want raspberry seeds in it, strain it through a food mill or sieve.

Raspberry Applesauce

MAKES 6 SERVINGS (½ CUP EACH)

4 large apples (about 6 ounces each), peeled, cored, and sliced

½ cup fresh raspberries

¾ cup water, divided

1 tablespoon ground cinnamon

½ teaspoon ground nutmeg

¼ cup Splenda No Calorie Sweetener

Mix the apples and raspberries with ½ cup water in a heavy saucepan. Stir in cinnamon, nutmeg, sweetener, and ¼ cup water.

Cover and cook over medium heat for 20 minutes or until apples are tender. Remove cover carefully, away from face, and stir once or twice while apples are cooking, adding small amounts of extra water if needed.

Cool applesauce and pour into a bowl. Mash sauce with a potato masher. Pour sauce into a covered container and refrigerate until ready to serve.

Per Serving: Calories: 70; % of calories from fat: 4; Fat (gm): 0.4; Saturated Fat (gm): 0.1; Cholesterol (mg): 0; Sodium (mg): 2; Protein (gm): 0.5; Carbohydrate (gm): 19.4 Exchanges: Milk: 0.0; Vegetable: 0.0; Fruit: 1.0; Bread: 0.0; Meat: 0.0; Fat: 0.0

Graham cracker crumbs are available at most large supermarkets. If they are not available, crush graham crackers between two sheets of waxed paper with a rolling pin, or crush them in a food processor or blender.

GRAHAM CRACKER CRUST

MAKES 1 (9-INCH) CRUST (8 SERVINGS)

4 tablespoons reduced-calorie margarine, melted
1 cup plus 2 tablespoons graham cracker crumbs

Preheat oven to 350°F.

Stir margarine and graham cracker crumbs together in a bowl. Press mixture firmly into the bottom and up the sides of a 9-inch pie pan.

Bake 10 minutes in center of oven, then remove to a wire rack to cool completely.

Per Serving: Calories: 85; % of calories from fat: 46; Fat (gm): 4.3; Saturated Fat (gm): 0.9; Cholesterol (mg): 0; Sodium (mg): 182; Protein (gm): 1.5; Carbohydrate (gm): 9.8 Exchanges: Milk: 0.0; Vegetable: 0.0; Fruit: 0.0; Bread: 0.5; Meat: 0.0; Fat: 1.0

SINGLE PIE CRUST

MAKES 1 (8-INCH) CRUST (8 SERVINGS)

1¼ cups all-purpose flour
2-inch strip tangerine, or orange, peel (white pith removed)
½ teaspoon salt
1 tablespoon plus 1 teaspoon butter, or vegetable shortening
¼–⅓ cup hot water

In a food processor, combine flour, tangerine peel, salt, and vegetable shortening and process until peel is finely minced, about 10 seconds. Add hot water through feed tube as processor is running, adding only enough water to make a soft dough. Gather dough into a ball. Chill for 20 minutes.

Refrigerate or freeze dough until ready to use. If frozen, remove from freezer 20 minutes before using.

Roll out dough on a lightly floured cloth to a circle about 10½ inches in diameter. Use as directed in recipe.

....

Per Serving: Calories: 88; % of calories from fat: 22; Fat (gm): 2.1; Saturated Fat (gm): 1.2; Cholesterol (mg): 5.1; Sodium (mg): 159; Protein (gm): 2; Carbohydrate (gm): 15 Exchanges: Milk: 0.0; Vegetable: 0.0; Fruit: 0.0; Bread: 1.0; Meat: 0.0; Fat: 0.5

Place crumbled gingersnap cookies between two sheets of waxed paper and crush, using a rolling pin; or crush them in a food processor or blender.

GINGERSNAP CRUST

MAKES 1 (9-INCH) PIE CRUST (8 SERVINGS)

4 tablespoons reduced-calorie margarine, or butter, melted

1 cup plus 2 tablespoons gingersnap crumbs

Preheat the oven to 350°F. Stir margarine and gingersnap crumbs together in a bowl. Press crumbs evenly over the bottom and up the sides of a 9-inch pie pan.

Bake crust in center of oven for 10 minutes. Remove from oven and cool before filling.

Instead of baking the crust, you can refrigerate it for at least 30 minutes.

Fill crust as directed in recipe.

....

Per Serving: Calories: 83; % of calories from fat: 45; Fat (gm): 4.2; Saturated Fat (gm): 0.9; Cholesterol (mg): 0; Sodium (mg): 161; Protein (gm): 0.8; Carbohydrate (gm): 10.8 Exchanges: Milk: 0.0; Vegetable: 0.0; Fruit: 0.0; Bread: 0.5; Meat: 0.0; Fat: 1.0

In the summer, you may wish to substitute fresh blueberries for the apples. Turnovers freeze well, making them great to have on hand for snacks or a quick dessert. Bake them straight from the freezer, adding a couple of minutes to the baking time.

FRUIT TURNOVERS

MAKES 6 PASTRIES (1 TURNOVER PER SERVING)

¾ cup reduced-fat (2%) small-curd cottage cheese

¾ cup peeled and chopped apples

½ cup Splenda No Calorie Sweetener, divided

¾ teaspoon vanilla extract

6 sheets fillo dough, room temperature

Butter-flavored cooking spray

In a bowl, stir together cottage cheese, apples, ¼ cup of sweetener, and vanilla. Set aside.

Arrange sheets of fillo dough on a work surface. Working quickly so dough will not dry out, cut each sheet lengthwise into 3 equal strips.

Preheat oven to 400°F. Spray a cookie sheet.

Spray 3 fillo strips and stack them on top of each other. Spoon about ¼ cup of filling onto bottom left corner of fillo stack. Fold the bottom right corner over the filling, then fold the filled corner up and to the right, and continue folding (as you would a flag) to make a triangular turnover. Set turnover on prepared cookie sheet. Continue until all the turnovers have been made.

Spray tops of turnovers. Sprinkle with remaining sweetener. Bake for 12 to 14 minutes or until golden on top. Serve warm or freeze.

··

Per Serving: Calories: 99; % of calories from fat: 16; Fat (gm): 1.9; Saturated Fat (gm): 0.7; Cholesterol (mg): 3; Sodium (mg): 245; Protein (gm): 6.6; Carbohydrate (gm): 15.3 Exchanges: Milk: 0.0; Vegetable: 0.0; Fruit: 0.0; Bread: 1.0; Meat: 0.0; Fat: 0.5

According to folklore, this recipe got its name because when the dough is added to the bubbling hot fruit, one can hear a grunting noise. I've never heard the grunt, but it's still a good story. Ask the children to listen for the grunt.

PEAR GRUNT

MAKES 8 SERVINGS

¾ cup all-purpose flour

¼ cup Splenda No Calorie Sweetener, or 3 tablespoons sugar, divided

1 teaspoon baking powder

3 tablespoons reduced-calorie margarine

3 tablespoons nonfat, or reduced-fat, milk

4 cups peeled, cored, and sliced ripe but firm pears (about 6 large)

¾ cup water

½ teaspoon ground cinnamon

Mix together flour, 1 tablespoon of sweetener, baking powder, margarine, and milk in a food processor. Process a few seconds to make a stiff dough. Set aside.

Stir together pear slices, remaining sweetener, water, and cinnamon in a medium saucepan. Bring fruit mixture to a boil over medium heat. Cook for 5 minutes, stirring once. Drop dough by the tablespoonful onto the hot, cooking fruit. Cover and continue cooking for 10 minutes or until dumplings are cooked through.

Spoon cooked fruit and a dumpling into each dessert dish. If desired, top with fat-free nondairy whipped topping or sugar-free vanilla ice cream. Serve immediately.

....

Per Serving: Calories: 112; % of calories from fat: 17; Fat (gm): 2.3; Saturated Fat (gm): 0.4; Cholesterol (mg): 0.1; Sodium (mg): 116; Protein (gm): 1.8; Carbohydrate (gm): 23 Exchanges: Milk: 0.0; Vegetable: 0.0; Fruit: 1.0; Bread: 0.5; Meat: 0.0; Fat: 0.5

Country Apple Pie

MAKES 8 SERVINGS

2 tablespoons reduced-fat margarine
Butter-flavored cooking spray
5 tablespoons Splenda No Calorie Sweetener, divided
1 teaspoon ground cinnamon
5 cups sliced firm apples, such as Granny Smith
1 recipe Single Pie Crust (see recipe on page 125)
1 egg white, lightly beaten

Melt margarine in a sprayed nonstick frying pan over medium heat. Stir in 4 tablespoons sweetener. Mix in cinnamon. Add apples and cook, stirring occasionally, until just fork tender, about 10 minutes. Remove from heat and let cool.

Preheat oven to 425°F.

On a lightly floured surface, roll out dough to a circle 10½ to 11 inches in diameter. Gently transfer dough to a nonstick cookie sheet. Arrange cooled apples in center of the dough, leaving a 1-inch rim of dough. Gather up edges to form a 1-inch dough perimeter. Pleat dough to form a rim. Alternately, for a traditionally shaped pie, use a sprayed pie pan.

Brush edges with egg white and sprinkle with remaining sweetener.

Bake in center of oven for 30 minutes or until crust is golden.

....

Per Serving: Calories: 139; % of calories from fat: 22; Fat (gm): 3.6; Saturated Fat (gm): 1.5; Cholesterol (mg): 5.1; Sodium (mg): 202; Protein (gm): 2.7; Carbohydrate (gm): 25.7 Exchanges: Milk: 0.0; Vegetable: 0.0; Fruit: 0.5; Bread: 1.0; Meat: 0.0; Fat: 0.5

Use chopped frozen fruit for a quick pie. Silky and rich, custard makes a good foil to the tartness of fruit.

CRUSTLESS CUSTARD FRUIT PIE

MAKES 8 SERVINGS

Butter-flavored cooking spray
2 cups frozen chopped peaches, pears, or apples, defrosted
2⅔ cups reduced-fat (2%) milk
⅔ cup all-purpose flour
½ cup Splenda No Calorie Sweetener
1½ teaspoons vanilla extract
½ cup egg substitute

Preheat oven to 375°F. Spray a 9-inch pie plate. Arrange peaches in bottom of pie plate.

In a bowl, whisk together milk, flour, sweetener, vanilla, and egg substitute. Pour custard mixture over peaches.

Bake pie in center of oven for 1 hour and 10 minutes or until custard has set and toothpick inserted in center comes out clean. Cool and serve. If not serving immediately, refrigerate.

....

Per Serving: Calories: 101; % of calories from fat: 15; Fat (gm): 1.7; Saturated Fat (gm): 1; Cholesterol (mg): 6.5; Sodium (mg): 62; Protein (gm): 5.5; Carbohydrate (gm): 16.6 Exchanges: Milk: 0.0; Vegetable: 0.0; Fruit: 0.0; Bread: 1.0; Meat: 0.0; Fat: 0.5

Star fruit, a shiny yellow, juicy fruit grown in the Caribbean, has an amazing star shape when cut crosswise.

STAR-TOPPED FRUIT SALAD

MAKES 6 SERVINGS

2 cups strawberries, hulled and sliced

1 cup raspberries

1 small cantaloupe, peeled and cut into small cubes, about

2 cups Splenda No-Calorie Sweetener, to taste

1 star fruit, sliced

Toss strawberries, raspberries, and cantaloupe in a large mixing bowl. Stir in sweetener. Chill until serving time.

Serve fruit in a shallow bowl or in individual glass salad bowls. Arrange star fruit slices on top.

Per Serving: Calories: 49; % of calories from fat: 7; Fat (gm): 0.4; Saturated Fat (gm): 0; Cholesterol (mg): 0; Sodium (mg): 10; Protein (gm): 1.2; Carbohydrate (gm): 11.5 Exchanges: Milk: 0.0; Vegetable: 0.0; Fruit: 1.0; Bread: 0.0; Meat: 0.0; Fat: 0.0

These tiny cheesecakes are just enough when you want a taste of something sweet.

No-Bake Strawberry Cheesecakes

MAKES 24 SMALL CHEESECAKES (1 PER SERVING)

CRUST:
  1 cup vanilla cookie crumbs
  2 tablespoons reduced-fat margarine, melted

CHEESECAKE FILLING:
  1 teaspoon unflavored gelatin
  1 tablespoon cold water
  1½ cups low-fat (2%) cottage cheese
  ¾ teaspoon vanilla extract
  ⅓ cup Splenda No-Calorie Sweetener

STRAWBERRY TOPPING:
  24 large strawberries, hulled
  1 packet sugar-free glaze

Arrange 24 mini-cupcake liners in miniature cupcake pan.

To Prepare Crust: Toss together vanilla cookie crumbs and margarine. Press crumbs in bottom of each cupcake liner. Set aside.

To Prepare Filling: Stir together gelatin and cold water in a small pan or microwave-proof glass cup. Let stand for 1 minute, until softened. Heat over medium-high heat for a couple of minutes or in the microwave on High, stirring once or twice, until gelatin is dissolved. Cool. In a food processor, puree cottage cheese, vanilla, and sweetener until smooth. Add gelatin with processor running, and process a few more seconds until mixture is smooth.

Pour filling into cupcake liners and refrigerate until set, about 3 to 4 hours.

To Prepare Topping: Place 1 strawberry on top of each mini-cheesecake. Prepare glaze according to package directions. Drizzle glaze over strawberry. Refrigerate until serving time.

....

Per Serving: Calories: 41; % of calories from fat: 33; Fat (gm): 1.6; Saturated Fat (gm): 0.5; Cholesterol (mg): 1.1; Sodium (mg): 81.9; Protein (gm): 2.3; Carbohydrate (gm): 4.8 Exchanges: Milk: 0.0; Vegetable: 0.0; Fruit: 0.0; Bread: 0.5; Meat: 0.0; Fat: 0.0

What fun having a great-tasting ice cream sandwich all ready for an after-school treat? By the time you arrive home from the supermarket, the ice cream is usually soft enough to make the sandwiches.

ICE CREAM SANDWICHES

MAKES 4 SANDWICHES

4 graham crackers
4 scoops (⅓ cup each) no-sugar-added and fat-free vanilla ice
cream, softened

Carefully break graham crackers along the break line making 8 cookies. Set aside.

Spread ⅓ cup of ice cream on one side of a cracker. Working quickly, place the remaining crackers on top of the ice cream. Squeeze down slightly so that the ice cream will spread to the edge of the crackers.

Cover each ice cream sandwich with plastic wrap and quickly put them in the freezer until ready to serve.

When ready to serve, remove Ice Cream Sandwiches from the freezer and discard wrappers.

....

Per Serving: Calories: 90; % of calories from fat: 7; Fat (gm): 0.7; Saturated Fat (gm): 0.1; Cholesterol (mg): 0.0; Sodium (mg): 76; Protein (gm): 2.5; Carbohydrate (gm): 18 Exchanges: Milk: 0.0; Vegetable: 0.0; Fruit: 0.0; Bread: 1.0; Meat: 0.0; Fat: 0.0

This is a fantastic way to use up leftover cooked rice and add a fine ending to a carefree meal. Or serve as an after-school snack.

THE QUICKEST RICE PUDDING

MAKES 12 SERVINGS (⅓ CUP PER SERVING)

1 package (1.4 ounces) instant vanilla sugar-free pudding mix

2 cups reduced-fat (2%) milk

2 cups cooked, cooled brown rice

½ teaspoon ground cinnamon

⅓ cup raisins, or dried cranberries, optional

Whisk together pudding mix and milk until smooth. Stir in rice, cinnamon, and raisins (if using).

Pour mixture into a bowl and let set for about 10 minutes. Spoon into individual pudding bowls and serve.

....

Per Serving: Calories: 67; % of calories from fat: 15; Fat (gm): 1.1; Saturated Fat (gm): 0.6; Cholesterol (mg): 3.3; Sodium (mg): 155; Protein (gm): 2.2; Carbohydrate (gm): 11.9 Exchanges: Milk: 0.0; Vegetable: 0.0; Fruit: 0.0; Bread: 1.0; Meat: 0.0; Fat: 0.0

Serve this as a dessert, a nutritious breakfast, a snack, or a side dish. Raisins or currants can be substituted for apricots.

INDIVIDUAL NOODLE PUDDINGS

MAKES 12 SERVINGS

Butter-flavored cooking spray

1½ cups nonfat cottage cheese

1 cup nonfat milk

½ cup Splenda No Calorie Sweetener, or sugar

½ cup egg substitute, or 2 eggs

1 teaspoon vanilla extract

8 ounces thin noodles, cooked according to package directions, drained, and cooled

6 ounces dried apricots, cut into thin strips

Preheat oven to 350°F. Spray a 12-cup nonstick muffin pan.

In a mixing bowl, combine cottage cheese, milk, sweetener, egg substitute, and vanilla. Stir in drained noodles and apricots.

Divide mixture evenly among prepared muffin cups. Bake in center of oven until knife inserted into center of a pudding comes out clean. Cool slightly.

To loosen puddings, run a knife around edges while they are still warm. Pry them out of the pan with a spoon. Serve warm or cold.

Per Serving: Calories: 140; % of calories from fat: 6; Fat (gm): 1; Saturated Fat (gm): 0.3; Cholesterol (mg): 26.2; Sodium (mg): 138; Protein (gm): 7.9; Carbohydrate (gm): 25.7 Exchanges: Milk: 0.0; Vegetable: 0.0; Fruit: 0.0; Bread: 2.0; Meat: 0.0; Fat: 0.0

This no-bake recipe is for Rebecca Hall, age 10, granddaughter of my oldest friend, Harriet.

BANANA CREAM PIE

MAKES 8 SERVINGS

1 Graham Cracker Crust (see recipe on page 124)

1½ cups sliced bananas (about 2 medium bananas)

1 package (1.4 ounces) instant fat-free, sugar-free banana pudding mix

2 cups nonfat milk

½ cup sugar-free, nondairy whipped topping

Prepare crust and set aside. Arrange sliced bananas on bottom of pie crust. Whisk pudding mix and milk together in a mixing bowl. Let stand 1 minute, then pour into pie crust over bananas.

Let pie firm up in refrigerator for about 10 minutes. Serve with whipped topping.

Per Serving: Calories: 144.4; % of calories from fat: 28; Fat (gm): 4.6; Saturated Fat (gm): 1.1; Cholesterol (mg): 1.2; Sodium (mg): 379; Protein (gm): 3.9; Carbohydrate (gm): 22.4 Exchanges: Milk: 0.0; Vegetable: 0.0; Fruit: 0.0; Bread: 1.5; Meat: 0.0; Fat: 1.0

Waffles can be made ahead of time, wrapped, and frozen for quick after-school treats or last-minute desserts. The warm waffles are good plain or with chopped fruit.

CHOCOLATE WAFFLES

MAKES 8 (4-INCH) WAFFLES (1 PER SERVING)

1½ cups all-purpose flour

½ cup unsweetened cocoa powder

¼ cup Splenda No Calorie Sweetener, or sugar

2 teaspoons baking powder

1 teaspoon baking soda

1½ cups nonfat buttermilk

¾ cup egg substitute, or 3 eggs

1 teaspoon vanilla extract

Whisk together all ingredients. Let batter stand for 15 minutes before using. Stir again before pouring.

Cook waffles in waffle iron according to manufacturer's instructions, usually using ⅓ cup batter per waffle.

Serve warm. According to taste, dust very lightly with confectioner's sugar, top with chopped fruit, or top with 1 small scoop (½ cup) of sugar-free vanilla ice cream.

....

Per Serving: Calories: 126; % of calories from fat: 6; Fat (gm): 1; Saturated Fat (gm): 0.5; Cholesterol (mg): 0.9; Sodium (mg): 343; Protein (gm): 7.2; Carbohydrate (gm): 24.6 Exchanges: Milk: 0.0; Vegetable: 0.0; Fruit: 0.0; Bread: 1.5; Meat: 0.0; Fat: 0.0

One can always add berries or chopped peaches or other peeled and chopped fruit to tapioca pudding.

VANILLA TAPIOCA PUDDING

MAKES 6 SERVINGS (½ CUP PER SERVING)

3½ tablespoons granulated tapioca
⅓ cup Splenda No Calorie Sweetener
¼ cup egg substitute, or 1 egg
3 cups reduced-fat (2%) milk
1½ teaspoons vanilla extract

In a medium saucepan, mix together tapioca, sweetener, egg substitute, and milk. Let stand 5 to 6 minutes. Stir again, then cook over medium-low heat for 20 minutes, stirring occasionally, until thickened. Mix in vanilla.

Cool and pour into individual dessert dishes.

Per Serving: Calories: 89; % of calories from fat: 23; Fat (gm): 2.4; Saturated Fat (gm): 1.5; Cholesterol (mg): 9.8; Sodium (mg): 69; Protein (gm): 5; Carbohydrate (gm): 12.3 Exchanges: Milk: 0.5; Vegetable: 0.0; Fruit: 0.0; Bread: 0.5; Meat: 0.0; Fat: 0.5

These "wormy" apples are especially fun for Halloween, though young children will enjoy them any time of year. Wooden craft sticks are available at hobby shops and stores that sell cooking supplies.

"WORMY" APPLES ON A STICK

MAKES 6 SERVINGS

> 6 firm medium apples, such as Golden Delicious, washed and dried
> 6 wooden craft sticks
> 6 sugar-free gummy worms

Insert a stick in blossom end of each apple. Arrange worm, attaching it on top of the stick so it wraps around apple.

....

Per Serving: Calories: 81; % of calories from fat: 2; Fat (gm): 0.2; Saturated Fat (gm): 0; Cholesterol (mg): 0; Sodium (mg): 1; Protein (gm): 0.4; Carbohydrate (gm): 23.3 Exchanges: Milk: 0.0; Vegetable: 0.0; Fruit: 1.5; Bread: 0.0; Meat: 0.0; Fat: 0.0

Chocolate in small amounts is a treat for any child, and some research now shows that chocolate (without a lot of sugar) is healthful.

APPLES ON A STICK DRIZZLED WITH CHOCOLATE

MAKES 6 SERVINGS

6 firm medium apples, such as Golden Delicious, washed and dried

6 wooden craft sticks

3 tablespoons melted semisweet chocolate

Insert a stick in blossom end of each apple.

Carefully spoon the chocolate into a small plastic sandwich bag. With scissors, snip off a very small corner of the bag. Squeeze chocolate into the corner of the bag below the snipped corner. Drizzle chocolate from the bag to create designs around each apple, using 1½ teaspoonfuls of chocolate per apple. Continue until all the apples have been decorated.

Place apples on a sheet of waxed paper until chocolate is set.

....

Per Serving: Calories: 92; % of calories from fat: 12; Fat (gm): 1.4; Saturated Fat (gm): 0.7; Cholesterol (mg): 0; Sodium (mg): 1; Protein (gm): 0.7; Carbohydrate (gm): 22 Exchanges: Milk: 0.0; Vegetable: 0.0; Fruit: 1.5; Bread: 0.0; Meat: 0.0; Fat: 0.0

Serve this sundae for a festive dessert or in meringue shells (see recipe on page 154) on special occasions.

STRAWBERRY SUNDAES

MAKES 4 SERVINGS

5 cups hulled, sliced strawberries
¾ cup Splenda No Calorie Sweetener, or sugar
¼ cup orange juice
4 scoops (½ cup each) sugar-free strawberry ice cream
4 tablespoons nondairy whipped topping

In a saucepan, mix together strawberries, sweetener, and orange juice. Simmer for 8 to 10 minutes or until berries are soft. Cool sauce.

For each sundae, place a scoop of ice cream in a sauce dish or parfait and drizzle with the strawberry sauce. Top with whipped topping. Serve immediately.

Per Serving: Calories: 162; % of calories from fat: 17; Fat (gm): 3.6; Saturated Fat (gm): 1.5; Cholesterol (mg): 10; Sodium (mg): 54; Protein (gm): 4.3; Carbohydrate (gm): 34.4 Exchanges: Milk: 0.0; Vegetable: 0.0; Fruit: 1.0; Bread: 1.0; Meat: 0.0; Fat: 0.5

These little cakes are just the right size for a child's tea party.

INDIVIDUAL CHOCOLATE CAKES

MAKES 20 CAKES (1 PER SERVING)

Butter-flavored cooking spray
1 package (18.25 ounces) super-moist chocolate cake mix
1⅓ cups water
¼ cup no-sugar-added applesauce
¼ cup canola oil
¾ cup egg substitute
7 tablespoons no-sugar-added raspberry preserves
60 almond slices

Preheat oven to 350°F. Spray a 7½ x 11-inch baking pan with butter-flavored cooking spray.

In a large bowl of electric mixer, beat together cake mix, 1⅓ cups water, applesauce, canola oil, and egg substitute. Mix for only 1 to 2 minutes; do not overbeat. Batter should be smooth.

Pour batter into pan, smoothing out top with spatula.

Bake in center of oven for 30 to 35 minutes or until cake tester or toothpick inserted in center of cake comes out clean. Cool. Carefully invert pan, and turn cake out onto clean surface. Using a 1½-inch-diameter cookie cutter, cut out cake rounds. Spoon 1 teaspoon of fruit preserves on top of each chocolate mini-cake. Sprinkle 3 almond slices on each cake.

....

Per Serving: Calories: 167; % of calories from fat: 37; Fat (gm): 7; Saturated Fat (gm): 1.3; Cholesterol (mg): 0; Sodium (mg): 192; Protein (gm): 3; Carbohydrate (gm): 24.1 Exchanges: Milk: 0.0; Vegetable: 0.0; Fruit: 0.0; Bread: 1.5; Meat: 0.0; Fat: 1.0

Consider this either a skinny flourless chocolate cake or a most delicious chocolate pancake. Freezes well.

FLOURLESS CHOCOLATE CAKE

MAKES 8 SERVINGS

Butter-flavored cooking spray
5 egg whites
4 ounces semisweet chocolate, chopped
3 tablespoons unsweetened cocoa
½ cup ground walnuts, almonds, or hazelnuts
½ cup Splenda No Calorie Sweetener
½ cup reduced-fat sour cream
½ cup egg substitute
½ teaspoon vanilla extract

Preheat oven to 350°F. Spray a 9-inch springform pan.

Beat egg whites in bowl of electric mixer on High until stiff, glossy peaks form. Set aside.

Microwave chocolate in microwave-safe bowl on High for 1 to 2 minutes. Stir until smooth. Scrape into a mixing bowl. Stir in cocoa, nuts, sweetener, sour cream, egg substitute, and vanilla. With spatula, fold in egg whites.

Spoon batter into prepared pan and gently smooth top. Bake in center of oven for 30 minutes. Cool. Loosen edges of pan and remove cake. Cake will deflate. This is great with a small (½ cup) scoop of sugar-free ice cream (not included in nutritional data).

....

Per Serving: Calories: 153; % of calories from fat: 53; Fat (gm): 10.5; Saturated Fat (gm): 3.7; Cholesterol (mg): 5.9; Sodium (mg): 70; Protein (gm): 6.7; Carbohydrate (gm): 13.7 Exchanges: Milk: 0.0; Vegetable: 0.0; Fruit: 0.0; Bread: 1.0; Meat: 0.0; Fat: 2.0

Do not let the yogurt get completely frozen. If you remove the yogurt cup and the yogurt is not completely chilled, return to the freezer until it is just right: firm but not too iced. Use any yogurt flavors your child likes; raspberry and key lime are popular.

FROZEN LEMON YOGURT

MAKES 1 SERVING

1 container (6 ounces) nonfat sugar-free lemon yogurt

Remove cover from yogurt container. Freeze yogurt for 1 hour. Remove yogurt from freezer and stir; it should be firm but not icy. If yogurt is not firm enough, return it to freezer for ½ hour and test again.

Per Serving: Calories: 67; % of calories from fat: 0; Fat (gm): 0; Saturated Fat (gm): 0; Cholesterol (mg): 3.7; Sodium (mg): 105; Protein (gm): 6; Carbohydrate (gm): 10.5 Exchanges: Milk: 1.0; Vegetable: 0.0; Fruit: 0.0; Bread: 0.0; Meat: 0.0; Fat: 0.0

Jelly beans add a bright splash of color to these easy-to-make tarts. If you don't have mini-tart pans, use a small regular tart pan (6 to 7 inches diameter).

Jelly Bean Tarts

MAKES 4 SERVINGS

> 4 metal mini-tart pans
>
> 8 tablespoons Graham Cracker Crust, unbaked (see recipe on page 124)
>
> 1 carton (8 ounces) light peach yogurt
>
> 12 sugar-free jelly beans

With clean hands or a teaspoon, press 2 tablespoons Graham Cracker Crust on bottom and up the sides of each pan.

Spoon 2 tablespoons of yogurt into each pan. It should come up to the top. Chill until serving time. Arrange 3 jelly beans decoratively on top of each tart.

....

Per Serving: Calories: 87; % of calories from fat: 24; Fat (gm): 2.5; Saturated Fat (gm): 0.7; Cholesterol (mg): 2.5; Sodium (mg): 116; Protein (gm): 2.3; Carbohydrate (gm): 15.3 Exchanges: Milk: 0.0; Vegetable: 0.0; Fruit: 0.0; Bread: 1.0; Meat: 0.0; Fat: 0.5

TOASTED ANGEL CAKE WITH RASPBERRIES

MAKES 8 SERVINGS

1 9-inch purchased angel cake
2⅔ cups fresh raspberries
Butter-flavored cooking spray
½ cup sugar-free nondairy whipped topping

Cut cake into 8 slices. In a bowl, crush raspberries with back of a spoon or fork. Spray a nonstick frying pan. Add cake and cook for about 1 minute, turning once, until cake is lightly toasted.

Place each warm slice of cake on an individual plate. Arrange berries over cake and top with a tablespoon of whipped topping.

Per Serving: Calories: 132; % of calories from fat: 5; Fat (gm): 0.7; Saturated Fat (gm): 0.1; Cholesterol (mg): 0; Sodium (mg): 320; Protein (gm): 3; Carbohydrate (gm): 29.6 Exchanges: Milk: 0.0; Vegetable: 0.0; Fruit: 1.0; Bread: 1.0; Meat: 0.0; Fat: 0.0

Rich and sweet without contributing sugar, these floats are a dream come true.

CREAM SODA FLOAT

MAKES 1 SERVING

1 scoop (½ cup) sugar-free vanilla ice cream

8 ounces sugar-free cream soda

Scoop vanilla ice cream into a tall glass. Slowly fill the glass with soda.

Serve immediately with a straw and spoon.

....

Per Serving: Calories: 100; % of calories from fat: 28; Fat (gm): 3; Saturated Fat (gm): 1.5; Cholesterol (mg): 10; Sodium (mg): 97; Protein (gm): 3; Carbohydrate (gm): 14 Exchanges: Milk: 0.0; Vegetable: 0.0; Fruit: 0.0; Bread: 1.0; Meat: 0.0; Fat: 0.5

What an adorable dessert for a tea party—for children or grownups.

TEA PARTY PEACH MELBA CAKES

MAKES 20 LITTLE CAKES (1 PER SERVING)

Butter-flavored nonstick spray

1 package (18.25 ounces) white moist supreme
cake mix

1¼ cups water

⅓ cup plain fat-free yogurt

4 egg whites

20 tablespoons nondairy whipped topping

1 cup frozen sliced peaches, defrosted

1 cup frozen raspberries, defrosted

Raspberry Sauce (recipe follows), optional

Preheat oven to 350°F. Spray a 7½ x 11-inch baking pan.

In a large bowl with an electric mixer, beat together cake mix, 1¼ cups water, yogurt, and egg whites. Mix only about 1 to 2 minutes; do not overbeat. Batter should be smooth.

Pour batter into pan, smoothing out top with spatula.

Bake in center of oven for 30 to 35 minutes or until cake tester or toothpick inserted in center of cake comes out clean. Cool.

Using a 2-inch round cookie cutter, cut out circles, and lift them out of pan gently, with a small spatula or knife.

To serve, place a cake on each dessert plate, drop a dollop of whipped topping over it, add peach slices, and sprinkle with raspberries. Drizzle with about 1 tablespoon of sauce, if using.

....

WITHOUT RASPBERRY SAUCE Per Serving: Calories: 129; % of calories from fat: 18; Fat (gm): 2.5; Saturated Fat (gm): 0.8; Cholesterol (mg): 0.1; Sodium (mg): 181; Protein (gm): 2.1; Carbohydrate (gm): 23.7 Exchanges: Milk: 0.0; Vegetable: 0.0; Fruit: 0.5; Bread: 1.0; Meat: 0.0; Fat: 0.5

Raspberry Sauce has many uses: try it on pancakes, French toast, or cut fresh fruit.
If sauce is too thick, simply add water or orange juice to desired thickness.

RASPBERRY SAUCE

MAKES 1 ½ CUPS (1 TO 2 TABLESPOONS PER SERVING)

2 packages (12 ounces each) no-sugar-added frozen raspberries,
   defrosted, including juice
¼ cup orange juice
2 tablespoons no-sugar-added raspberry preserves

In a saucepan, heat the raspberries, orange juice, and raspberry preserves
over medium heat. Bring mixture to a boil and reduce heat to a simmer.
Continue simmering, stirring often, until mixture thickens slightly.

Cool, pour into a bowl, cover, and refrigerate until ready to serve.

RASPBERRY SAUCE ONLY Per Serving: Calories: 19; % of calories from fat: 0.4; Fat (gm): 0;
Saturated Fat (gm): 0; Cholesterol (mg): 0; Sodium (mg): 0; Protein (gm): 0.3; Carbohydrate
(gm): 4.5 Exchanges: Milk: 0.0; Vegetable: 0.0; Fruit: 0.0; Bread: 0.0; Meat: 0.0; Fat: 0.0

Wiggly, Slimy, Wormy Gelatin

MAKES 4 SERVINGS (½ CUP PER SERVING)

1 package lime-flavored sugar-free gelatin dessert
1 cup fresh, or frozen, defrosted, peaches, peeled and roughly
 chopped
8 sugar-free gummy worms

Put gelatin in a glass bowl. Stir in 1 cup of hot water. Whisk ingredients together until dissolved. Add 1 cup minus 1 tablespoon water, and blend together.

Cool and place in refrigerator for 1 to 1½ hours until gelatin begins to set.

Mix in peaches and gummy worms. Return to refrigerator and allow gelatin to set, maybe 1 more hour.

To serve, spoon or cut gelatin into squares and place a serving on each dessert dish, making sure each child gets 2 worms.

Per Serving: Calories: 57; % of calories from fat: 3; Fat (gm): 0.2; Saturated Fat (gm): 0; Cholesterol (mg): 0; Sodium (mg): 60; Protein (gm): 1.8; Carbohydrate (gm): 14.5 Exchanges: Milk: 0.0; Vegetable: 0.0; Fruit: 1.0; Bread: 0.0; Meat: 0.0; Fat: 0.0

WAFFLE SCOOPS AND PLUM SAUCE

MAKES 6 SERVINGS

3 cups chopped canned plums in juice
2 tablespoons Splenda No Calorie Brown Sugar Blend
¼ cup orange juice
6 warm Chocolate Waffles (see recipe page 137)

Using a small saucepan, sauté plums with Splenda Brown Sugar Blend and orange juice over medium heat, stirring often. Continue cooking until plums cook down and thicken into a thick sauce. Spoon sauce into a serving bowl.

Cut waffles into about 8 pieces each. Serve 1 cup up waffle on each dessert plate, and place the bowl of plum sauce in the middle of the table. Using fingers or fork, depending on age of child, instruct children to scoop up plum sauce with pieces of waffle.

....

Per Serving: Calories: 214; % of calories from fat: 4; Fat (gm): 1; Saturated Fat (gm): 0.5; Cholesterol (mg): 0.9; Sodium (mg): 345; Protein (gm): 7.9; Carbohydrate (gm): 46.8 Exchanges: Milk: 0.0; Vegetable: 0.0; Fruit: 1.0; Bread: 2.0; Meat: 0.0; Fat: 0.0

Let the children celebrate Presidents' Day by inviting friends over, and perhaps let them help make and enjoy this cherry treat.

WASHINGTON'S BIRTHDAY CHERRY TREAT

MAKES 6 SERVINGS

⅓ cup uncooked quick-cooking oatmeal

¼ cup all-purpose flour

¼ cup Splenda Brown Sugar Blend

½ teaspoon pie spice mix

¼ cup reduced-fat margarine, room temperature

1 can (16 ounces) tart red cherries in water, including liquid

1 cup frozen unsweetened strawberries, defrosted

Preheat oven to 400°F. Use an 8 x 8-inch baking pan.

In a medium bowl, whisk together, oatmeal, flour, Splenda, and spice mix. Cut in margarine until mixture resembles coarse crumbs.

Put cherries and strawberries in a separate bowl. Toss crumb mixture with fruit.

Spoon fruit and crumb mixture evenly in pan.

Bake in center of oven for 15 minutes or until fruit is bubbly and crumbs toasted.

Cool. When easy to serve, divide into individual dessert bowls or custard cups.

....

Per Serving: Calories: 126; % of calories from fat: 30; Fat (gm): 4.2; Saturated Fat (gm): 0.8; Cholesterol (mg): 0; Sodium (mg): 98.3; Protein (gm): 2; Carbohydrate (gm): 20.1 Exchanges: Milk: 0.0; Vegetable: 0.0; Fruit: 1.0; Bread: 0.5; Meat: 0.0; Fat: 0.5

Dessert Pizza

MAKES 16 SERVINGS

Butter-flavored cooking spray

1 recipe Whole-Wheat Pizza Crust (see recipe page 137)

5 cups peeled and thinly sliced cooking apples, such as Granny
Smith or Golden Delicious

3 tablespoons lemon juice

¼ cup Splenda Brown Sugar Blend

2 teaspoons pie spice mix

Preheat oven to 425°F. Spray cookie sheet.

With very clean, floured hands, push dough (or roll it out) evenly into two
circles, each about 9 to 10 inches in diameter. Place crusts on prepared
pan.

Put apples in a bowl. Toss with lemon juice, Splenda brown sugar blend,
and pie spice.

Spray crusts. Arrange apples over crusts. Form a rim around the perimeter
with ½ inch of dough.

Bake pizza on top shelf of oven until crusts are firm and apples hot, about
20 minutes.

....

Per Serving: Calories: 107; % of calories from fat: 1; Fat (gm): 1.2; Saturated Fat (gm): 0.2;
Cholesterol (mg): 0; Sodium (mg): 74.3; Protein (gm): 2.6; Carbohydrate (gm): 21.9 Exchanges:
Milk: 0.0; Vegetable: 0.0; Fruit: 0.5; Bread: 1.0; Meat: 0.0; Fat: 0.0

To change the flavor to vanilla, omit the mint flavoring and substitute 1 teaspoon of vanilla. To make green mint meringues, just add 2 to 3 drops of green food coloring. Fun for Christmas!

MINT MERINGUE SHELLS FOR CHRISTMAS

MAKES 8 SHELLS (1 SHELL PER SERVING)

Butter-flavored cooking spray
6 egg whites
1 teaspoon cream of tartar
¾ cup Splenda No Calorie Sweetener
1 teaspoon mint extract

Preheat oven to 225°F. Spray a cookie sheet lined with aluminum foil.

With an electric mixer, beat egg whites until soft peaks form. Sprinkle with cream of tartar and sweetener. Beat until stiff, glossy peaks form. Mix in mint flavoring.

Scoop meringue out of mixing bowl with a ½-cup measuring cup. Set meringues on prepared cookie sheet. Use back of tablespoon to make a depression in center of each shell.

Bake meringue shells undisturbed in center of oven for 1 hour or until dry. Turn off oven and leave shells undisturbed overnight in the oven with door shut. The shells should be crisp and firm.

Carefully remove shells with spatula to serving plates. They crumble easily so handle carefully. If they crumble, just fill a small cup with meringue crumbs and let the children enjoy them.

....

Per Serving: Calories: 16; % of calories from fat: 2; Fat (gm): 0.1; Saturated Fat (gm): 0; Cholesterol (mg): 0; Sodium (mg): 42; Protein (gm): 2.7; Carbohydrate (gm): 2.7 Exchanges: Milk: 0.0; Vegetable: 0.0; Fruit: 0.0; Bread: 0.0; Meat: 0.0; Fat: 0.0

CRUNCHY VANILLA COOKIES FOR AFTER-SCHOOL SNACKING

MAKES 20 COOKIES (2 PER SERVING)

Butter-flavored cooking spray
¾ cup egg substitute
⅓ cup Splenda No Calorie Sweetener, or sugar
3 tablespoons vegetable shortening
1 teaspoon vanilla extract
1½ cups all-purpose flour
1 teaspoon baking powder
½ cup currants, or dried cranberries

Preheat oven to 350°F. Spray a nonstick cookie sheet.

Using large bowl of electric mixer, combine egg substitute and Splenda. Beat in shortening, vanilla extract, flour, and baking powder. Stir in currants.

Divide dough in half. On the cookie sheet, form each half into a log shape about 2 inches in diameter.

Bake in center of oven for 20 to 25 minutes. Logs will be firm to the touch and slightly golden.

Using pot holders, remove pan from oven. With a small sharp knife, cut logs into about ⅓ –inch-thick slices. Bake slices for 4 to 5 minutes longer or until they are just crisp. Cool.

Per Serving: Calories: 57; % of calories from fat: 30; Fat (gm): 1.9; Saturated Fat (gm): 0.5; Cholesterol (mg): 0; Sodium (mg): 42; Protein (gm): 1.9; Carbohydrate (gm): 8.2 Exchanges: Milk: 0.0; Vegetable: 0.0; Fruit: 0.0; Bread: 0.5; Meat: 0.0; Fat: 0.5

Here is an update on everyone's favorite: the oatmeal cookie. They are great to put in the lunch box. Put in extra ones to give to friends, too.

OATMEAL NUGGETS

MAKES 18 NUGGETS (2 PER SERVING)

½ cup reduced-fat margarine

⅓ cup Splenda No Calorie Sweetener

1 teaspoon vanilla extract

¼ cup egg substitute

1½ cups all-purpose flour

½ cup quick-cooking oatmeal, uncooked

2 teaspoons baking powder

⅓ cup currants, raisins, or chopped walnuts

Butter-flavored cooking spray

Using the large bowl of electric mixer, mix together the margarine, Splenda, vanilla, and egg substitute. Blend in flour, oatmeal, baking powder, and currants. Roll dough into a ball. Cover with aluminum foil or plastic wrap. Refrigerate for 2 to 4 hours.

When ready to bake, preheat oven to 375°F. Spray a cookie sheet. Let dough stand at room temperature until pliable, about 10 minutes. Shape dough into ¾-inch balls. Set dough balls on prepared cookie sheet.

Bake nuggets in center of oven for 7 to 10 minutes or until they are just firm and golden color. Cool.

....

Per Serving: Calories: 72; % of calories from fat: 33; Fat (gm): 2.7; Saturated Fat (gm): 0.5; Cholesterol (mg): 0; Sodium (mg): 122; Protein (gm): 1.8; Carbohydrate (gm): 10.4 Exchanges: Milk: 0.0; Vegetable: 0.0; Fruit: 0.0; Bread: 0.5; Meat: 0.0; Fat: 0.5

Use this recipe for a festive dessert, especially when you are serving Mexican food. Custard is served upside down so that it has a sweet topping.

FLAN

MAKES 6 SERVINGS

¼ cup sugar

¼ cup Splenda No Calorie Sweetener

1¾ cups reduced-fat (2%) milk

½ cup egg substitute

1 teaspoon vanilla extract

Preheat oven to 350°F. Have 6 custard cups and a roasting pan available.

In a small saucepan, heat ¼ cup of sugar over low heat, stirring constantly until it is just beginning to turn a golden color. Add 1½ teaspoons hot water. Continue simmering and stirring until sugar is a caramel color. Spoon equal amounts of mixture into the custard cups. Set aside.

In a small bowl, combine the Splenda, milk, egg substitute, and vanilla. Pour equal amounts of custard mixture into the cups.

Set filled cups in the roasting pan. Put pan in oven. Using a pitcher, pour water gently into the roasting pan until it comes half-way up sides of custard cups.

Bake Flan for 1 hour. Custard will be set, wiggly but not loose. A knife inserted in the center will come out clean and dry. Cool Flan on a rack. Refrigerate at least 3 to 4 hours before serving.

When ready to serve, loosen custard from custard cups by running a small knife around each custard. Place a dessert plate on top of each custard cup and invert Flan onto it.

....

Per Serving: Calories: 79; % of calories from fat: 15; Fat (gm): 1.4; Saturated Fat (gm): 0.9; Cholesterol (mg): 5.7; Sodium (mg): 67.6; Protein (gm): 4.3; Carbohydrate (gm): 12.8 Exchanges: Milk: 0.0; Vegetable: 0.0; Fruit: 0.0; Bread: 1.0; Meat: 0.0; Fat: 0.0

INDEX

A

Angel Cake, Toasted, with
 Raspberries, 146
Apple Betty Pie, 122
Apple Pie, Country, 129
Apples, "Wormy," on a Stick, 139
Apples on a Stick Drizzled with
 Chocolate, 140
Applesauce, Raspberry, 123

B

Banana Cream Pie, 136
Banana-Stuffed French Toast, 34
Berry Sauce, 36
Blueberry Muffins wih Bunny
 Ears, 112
Blueberry Salad, 70
Burger, Grilled, with All the
 Trimmings, 100

C

Cake
 After-School Snacking, 25
 Angel, Toasted, with
  Raspberries, 146
 Chocolate, Flourless, 143
 Chocolate, Individual, 142
 Peach Melba, Tea Party, 148
 Yellow, Lunch Box, 27
California Rolls with Turkey, 110
Cantaloupe Soup in a Shell, 87
Carbohydrate counting, xi
Carrot Quiche, Crustless, 43
Cereal Toss, 15
Cheesecake, Strawberry, No-
 Bake, 132
Cheese

Roll-Ups, 3
 Sandwich, Grilled, 60
Cherry Cupcakes, 117
Cherry Treat, Washington's
 Birthday, 152
Chicken
 Aloha, 108
 Campfire, and Roasted
  Potatoes, 95
 Fajitas, 62
 Greek, 99
 Nugget Strips, 13
 with Rice, 94
 Rotisserie, Customized, 102
 Sausages with Apples, 106
 "Wings," 11
Chili Soup, 89
Chili Spice, 95
Chili, Turkey, Cowboy Bill's, 106
Chips, Sweet Potato with Salsa,
 21
Chocolate
 Cake, Flourless, 143
 Cake, Individual, 142
 Chip Muffin Tops, 114
 Cupcakes, Mini, 118
 Drizzled Apples on a Stick,
  140
 Waffles, 137
Chutney, Pineapple, Grilled Fruit
 Salad with, 73, 74
Cocoa Muffins, 113
Coleslaw, Nutty, 78
Cookies
 Crunchy, Vanilla, 155
 Oatmeal Nuggets, 156
Corn off the Cob, Tossed, 80

Crepes, 39
Crust
 Graham Cracker, 124
 Pie, 125
 Pie, Gingersnap, 126
 Pizza, 47
Cupcakes
 Angel, 116
 Cherry, 117
 Ice Cream Cone, 119
 Mini Chocolate,118
Custard Fruit Pie, 130

D

Dept. of Agriculture, U.S.,
 standards, xii
Desserts, 121–157
Diabetes
 and children, ix
 and diet, ix–xi
 information on, ix–xi
Dip, Island Fruit, 20
Dressing, Green, 71

E

Egg(s) and Egg Substitute
 Breakfast A-Go Go, 40
 Chinese, 32
 in a Hole, 33
 with Lox and Onion, 98
 Salad Stuffed in a Horn, 67
 Scrambled Whites, 10
 Tortilla Wrap, Southwest
  Scrambled, 60
English muffins, 4
Exchange system, diabetes, xi

F

Fajitas, Chicken, 62
Fish Strips, 104
Flan, 157
Float, Cream Soda, 147
Food Guide Pyramid, x
French Toast, Banana-Stuffed, 34
French Toast, with Berry Sauce, 35
Frittata, Veggie, 98
Fruit
Dip, 20
Grilled, 18
Peaches in Blankets, 41
Pie, Custard, 130
Pineapple, 19
Salad, Grilled, with Pineapple Chutney, 73, 74
Salad, Star-Topped, 131
Turnovers, 127

G

Gelatin, Wiggly, Slimy, Wormy, 150
Gingersnap Pie Crust, 126
Graham Cracker Crust, 124
Grilled Cheese Sandwich, 60
Grits, 51
Grunt, Pear, 128

I, J, L

Ice Cream Sandwiches, 133
Ingredients, dietetic, xii
Jelly Bean Tarts, 145
Johnny Cakes, 7
Lox and Onion with Eggs, 99

M

Macaroni, Elbow, Salad, 54
Marinara Sauce, 56
Meal planning, xi, xii
Meatballs, Dinosaur, 93
Meringue Shells, Mint, 154
Muffin(s)
Blueberry, with Bunny Ears, 112
Cocoa, 113
English, 4
Tops, Chocolate Chip, 114

Munchies, 24

N

Nachos Grandes, 26
Noodle Pudding, Stir-Fried, 79
Noodle Puddings, Individual, 135
Noodles with Marinara Sauce, 55
Nutritional data, xi–xiii
(also see each recipe)

O

Oatmeal Nuggets, 156
Onion and Lox with Eggs, 99
Orzo Salad, 52

P

Pancakes
Puffy German, 31
Spud, with Sour Cream, 42
Vegetable, 30
Pasta
Angel Hair, Molded, 50
Macaroni, Elbow, Salad, 54
Noodles with Marinara Sauce, 55
Orzo Salad, 52
Pinenutty Thai, 57
Tortellini, Fried, 92
Ziti with Tomato Sauce, 53
Peach Melba Cakes, Tea Party, 148
Peaches in Blankets, 41
Peanut Butter and Jelly Pretzel Nuggets, 8
Pear Grunt, 128
Peas, Mushy, 83
Pie
Apple Betty, 122
Apple, Country, 129
Banana Cream, 136
Crust, 125
Crust, Gingersnap, 126
Crust, Graham Cracker, 124
Custard Fruit, 139
Pineapple Chutney, Grilled Fruit Salad with, 73, 74
Pineapple Slices, 19

Pitas, Suffed Mini, 9
Pizza, 2, 5, 46–49
Christmas Trees, 48
Crust, 47
Cut-Outs, 46
Dessert, 153
Mexican, 49
Popcorn, 23
Popcorn Soup, Tomato, 85
Popovers, 115
Popsicles, Frozen Fudge, 16
Potato(es)
Baked, 101
Pancakes with Sour Cream, 42
Roasted, 96
Roasted, and Campfire Chicken, 95
Salad, White and Green, 75
Pudding
Noodle, Individual, 135
Noodle, Stir-Fried, 79
Rice, Quickest, 134
Tapioca, Vanilla, 138

Q

Quesadillas, Shrimp, 63
Quesadillas, Turkey, 64
Quiche, Carrot, Crustless, 43

R

Ranch Sauce, 12
Raspberries, Toasted Angel Cake with, 146
Raspberry Applesauce, 123
Raspberry Sauce, 149
Rice with Chicken, 94
Rice Pudding, Quickest, 134

S

Salad
Blueberry, 70
Egg, Stuffed in a Horn, 67
Elbow Macaroni, 54
Far East in Radicchio Cups, 72
Fruit, with Pineapple Chutney, 73, 74

Fruit, Star-Topped, 131
Garbage, 68
Orzo, 52
Potato, White and Green, 75
Taco, 69
Thai, 76
Salsa, Fresh Tomato, 22
Sandwiches 60, 65
Sandwiches, Ice Cream, 133
Sauce
Berry, 36
Marinara, 56
Ranch, 12
Raspberry, 149
Sausages, Chicken, with Apples, 107
Sausages, Turkey, Homemade, 108
Scrambled Eggs, 10
Shells, Mint Meringue, 154
Shrimp Quesadillas, 63
Shrimp on a Stick, 82
Sloppy Joes, Gooey, 65
Slush (Juicicles), 17
Snacks, 1–27
Soda, Cream, Float, 147

Soup
Cantaloupe, in a Shell, 87
Chili, 89
10-Minute Popeye, 86
Tomato Popcorn, 85
Won Ton, 88
Strawberry Cheescake, No-Bake, 132
Strawberry Sundaes, 141
Sweet Potato Chips with Salsa, 21
Sweet Potatoes, Baked, 81

T
Taco Salad, 69
Tapioca Pudding, Vanilla, 138
Tarts, Jelly Bean, 145
Toast, Cinnamon, 6
Tomato Popcorn Soup, 85
Tomato Salsa, 22
Tortellini, Fried, 92
Trail Mix, 14
Tuna Roll, Rocky Shore, 66
Turkey
Chili, Cowboy Bill's, 105
Pick-Up Sticks, 103

Quesadillas, 64
Sausages, Homemade, 107
California Rolls with, 110
Turnovers, Fruit, 127

V
Vanilla Cookies, Crunchy, 155
Vegetables, Stir-Fried, 84
Veggie Frittata, 97

W
Waffle(s)
Buttermilk, 37
Chocolate, 137
Nutty, 38
Scoops and Plum Sauce, 151
"Wings," Chicken, 11
Won Ton Soup, 88

Y, Z
Yogurt, Lemon, Frozen, 144
Ziti with Tomato Sauce, 53

ABOUT THE AUTHOR

A former food columnist for the Chicago Sun-Times and the author of more than 50 cookbooks—including four for people with diabetes—Barbara Grunes is also a food historian and restaurant consultant. She lives in Chicago.